Mom's Got Money

A Millennial Mom's Guide to Managing
Money Like a Boss

Catherine Alford

For general information on our other products and services or for technical support,
please contact our Customer Care Department within the United States at (800)
762-2974, outside the United States at (317) 572-3993, or fax (317) 572-4002.

Wiley publishes in a variety of print and electronic formats and by print-on-demand.
Some material included with standard print versions of this book may not be included
in e-books or in print-on-demand. If this book refers to media such as a CD or DVD that
is not included in the version you purchased, you may download this material at http://
booksupport.wiley.com. For more information about Wiley products, visit www.wiley
.com.

Library of Congress Cataloging-in-Publication Data is available:

9781119759256(paperback)
9781119759324(epdf)
9781119759188(epub)

COVER DESIGN: PAUL McCARTHY
COVER ART: © JULIA TIM / SHUTTERSTOCK | PAUL McCARTHY
AUTHOR PHOTO: © JONATHAN ALFORD

SKY10025647_031721

This one's for me and for any other mom ready to give up.
Keep going.

Contents

Acknowledgments

I want to start by thanking my husband, Jonathan, because without him, this book would not exist. Jonathan, from the very beginning you encouraged me to pursue this goal. You supported me through every setback over the many years it took to make this dream a reality. I completed it with your help, your snacks, and all those walks you took with the kids so I could write. I wouldn't be a mom without you, and I certainly wouldn't be an author without you either. I love you!

Thank you to the entire team at Wiley, especially Kevin Harreld, for believing in this project and helping turn it into a finished product. Thank you to the Knight Agency, especially my literary agent, Elaine Spencer, for your brilliance, tenacity, and for figuring out how to sell my book.

Thank you to Jennifer Locke, for helping me create the perfect title for this book as well as Meghan Stevensen and Farnoosh Torabi, who helped bring my initial ideas together several years ago. Thanks also to Adam Kirschner for helping me grow my career in a meaningful way.

A special thank-you to my friend Katie Gilbert, who saw a tweet from my literary agency saying they were looking for writers in the personal finance niche and passed it along to me. Katie also spent time reading and editing this book when I finished, and her feedback gave me enough confidence to actually turn it in.

To Andrew Dewar, it's hard to adequately thank you in words. Your friendship and kindness is unparalleled. I don't know how many pep talks you had to give me while I wrote this book, but they certainly helped get it done. Also, thank you for reading this before I turned it in. You've secured your spot in the Top 5.

Thank you to the FinCon community, of which there are far too many people to name. You've been with me since my business and blog were in their infancy and have supported me with press, media mentions, podcast interviews, referrals, ideas, camaraderie, and wonderful friendships.

Thank you to my blog readers, my Instagram community, and every single supporter I've had along the way. Without your interest in what I do, this book would never be possible. Thank you for providing a platform for me to share my money stories and for all your encouragement.

Thank you to my parents, who instilled a love of reading in me from a very early age and encouraged my writing. Thank you for always buying me books—I realize now what a gift that was. My siblings and in-laws were also great cheerleaders. Mr. Darryl, thank you for reading everything I've written from the very beginning. You're the inspiration for many of my money choices. I love all of you.

A couple of other people provided great emotional support, advice, and ideas throughout this process: Katie Houf, Kristen Simmer, Jessi Fearon, Melody Zoma, Bola Sokunbi, Jason Vitug, Jason Brown, Andy Hill, Renee Sorgi, and Sara Levitsky.

Lastly, to Aria and Edison, my quarantine buddies, thank you for inspiring me to be better every day. Thank you for asking how many words I'd written that day and for always having hugs and kisses for me. It was a wild ride, and you got a ton of iPad time so I could write this book during a pandemic. We got through it together, though, didn't we? You were both so proud and excited for me when I told you I was finished with my book. I won't ever forget it. Remember, Alfords don't quit.

About the Author

Catherine Alford is a nationally recognized financial educator who helps moms recapture their life passions, earn more, and take on a more active financial role in their families. Catherine started her business as a personal blog with a $10 domain name in 2010. She then grew it into a multifaceted, six-figure digital media company that includes several personal finance websites, a suite of financial education products, and services that include financial writing, public speaking, and influencer marketing. Through her work, she partners with top financial companies as a speaker, video talent, and scriptwriter—all with the goal of helping women become more financially confident. Over the years, her writing and expertise have been featured in dozens of media outlets including *Good Morning America*, *Yahoo Finance*, *U.S. News and World Report*, *Real Simple*, *The Huffington Post*, *Kiplinger*, *Investopedia*, *Business Insider*, and many more. She currently lives just outside of Detroit, Michigan with her husband, their boy/girl twins, and a rescue dog named Julep. Learn more about Catherine at www.CatherineAlford.com.

Introduction

There's something you should know about the book you have in your hands: I fought really hard to get it to you. In fact, the process from the moment I created my book proposal to when I actually got a yes from a publisher took 4.5 years and 27 rejections. There were many times I wanted to give up and quit, but I kept thinking about you.

Yes, you.

I felt like if I quit on my idea, then I'd be quitting on you too. If I didn't try again after the fourteenth publisher said no or after the twentieth one said no, then you wouldn't get to meet me on these pages, and I wouldn't be able to encourage you to become a boss with your money.

So, I kept trying.

I don't want to make it sound like a movie with inspirational music playing in the background as I braved the world of rejection in publishing with strength against all odds. There were lots of doubts and an incalculable amount of tears along the way. I even took a four-month break in there when I didn't pitch this book at all because I needed a minute to regroup.

And yet, here we are.

That's something you'll come to know about me. I don't give up easily. And here's the best part: I won't let you give up on yourself either.

It doesn't matter how many times you've overspent. It doesn't matter how much debt you're in. I don't care if you've tried budgeting a thousand times and failed. I believe in you, and I know you can win.

I know you're overwhelmed with everything you have to manage on a day-to-day basis as a mom. But, you and I are not quitters. Through this book, I'm going to encourage you to keep going. It's never too late to get your money right and it's never too late to learn something new. I really believe that, and I'm so glad you're here so we can get started on the journey—together.

There's something else I want you to know. I wrote this book during the Covid-19 quarantine. In fact, I had my first call with my publisher on March 11, 2020 to discuss the process, and on March 13, 2020, I picked up my twins from kindergarten not knowing I wouldn't bring them back to school for more than six months.

I had grand visions of writing this book in darling coffee shops while I sipped a latte. My plan was to write half of it by the time my kids finished kindergarten. Then, I'd put the finishing touches on it while they had fun in camp over the summer. But then, the world closed. Schools closed. Coffee shops closed. And then camps closed.

My husband, who was a physician in residency training when I got my book deal, spent long hours at the hospital working the front lines of the pandemic. Then, he graduated from residency in July 2020 and moved four hours away to complete a one-year fellowship. It was always the plan for him to go away for a year of extra training, but we made that plan when I thought I'd have access to school, babysitters, camp, and my gym (with the super-fun childcare area).

Suffice to say, I faced many challenges when it came to writing this book, and I'm sure you can relate, because the world completely changed for every single one of us. Maybe you were home with your spouse during the quarantine. Maybe you were an essential worker and wished you could be home with your kids. Maybe you are a single mom and had childcare constraints as you tried to navigate the seemingly endless days. As for me, I ended up writing this book in little pockets of the day between kindergarten Zoom calls and using lots of bribery and too much iPad time to accomplish my mission.

At night, I'd be so exhausted I would use the voice-to-text function on my computer to write. Then, inevitably, one of my kids would need something in the night, and I'd wake up to find words like "Mama, Mama, Mama" inside my book because I'd abandoned my computer but left voice-to-text on. One time, I came back to my computer to find an entire paragraph about opening popsicles that voice-to-text recorded. I tell you this because although this book will go through rigorous editing, if you find a random "Mama" in the paragraphs, that's why.

Writing during a pandemic also fundamentally changed some of my beliefs about money, especially concerning emergency funds.

There were also certain stories in the book that didn't seem to fit anymore once I started to hear from people who were suffering. Some stories I initially shared seemed too happy, too inconsequential, or too tone-deaf during a global emergency. I got email after email from people struggling, people losing their jobs, and moms who were deeply unhappy because they were managing the brunt of the labor at home. I've done my best to find some balance, to be empathetic but also offer a little encouraging push in case you need one. I think mindset is everything, and I know that stepping into a boss mindset and taking control of your finances—even if you've been knocked to the ground during the pandemic—is the first step to recovery.

That said, I am not a financial planner (or a therapist). I became a part of the finance world when I started writing a blog about my life on a very tight graduate school budget in 2010. That budgeting blog blossomed into a freelance writing business when I started writing financial articles for other blogs and financial companies. Eventually, my business grew to include scriptwriting, video content, influencer work, speaking, and now—writing a book.

(Disclaimer: Although I've worked with dozens of financial companies through my business, some of which I mention in this book, none of them paid me to be mentioned here. I've also included studies and information from companies I haven't worked with in this book.)

Even though I didn't go to school for finance, I think the reason my budgeting blog and eventual financial writing business grew is because of how I write about money. I usually include relatable stories in my work, and because I'm not writing from some high-up place on Wall Street, I think it helps my readers easily understand some money concepts. I hope that's the case for you too.

My ability to write comes from a lifetime of pursuing writing and reading as my greatest passions. I went to college and graduate school for history because I was captivated by people's stories. I love learning about why humans make the choices they do, which is why the behavioral finance aspect of money is so fascinating to me.

My training as a researcher and historian came in handy when my writing clients assigned me articles about topics like mortgages and investing. Even if I didn't know the answers at first, I knew exactly how to find them. And, it wouldn't be long before I went down a rabbit hole researching the history of various industries and companies.

The Greek word *historia* means "inquiry." I always want to know why. Why are things the way they are? Why do people do what they do? Why are some people paid more than others? Why does money have such an impact? What can we learn from past choices? How can our past money choices empower and inform our future ones?

Think about it; money is this one singular object that has impacted history probably more than anything else. It's caused wars, death, shaped politics, and impacted populations for a lifetime. Money has also had life-changing positive impacts on the world through charitable gifts, eradication of disease, and aid.

But, money is not equal. For centuries, certain sectors of the population—namely women and the Black community—have not had equal opportunities when it comes to banking, homeownership, access to business loans, and investing. The result is not only a wage gap but a *wealth* gap.

And yet, I keep seeing seeds of hope. Every day, I meet new members of the financial community working hard to inspire positive change. I see women encouraging other women to speak up, ask for raises, and so many of us are teaching one another what it means to invest and to create generational wealth.

As a financial educator, I work hard to make the language of money more accessible to all. I want to encourage moms like you to feel like bosses and become a powerful force, so you can fearlessly ask questions about budgeting, salaries, investments, fees, homeownership, and more. The tides are changing, and moms are perfectly prepared to lead the charge and help their families attain financial success.

At the end of the day, money is just currency. It's just some pieces of paper or numbers on a screen. The money itself means nothing. It's the person holding it who assigns it value and gives it life. You can make a choice when you hold your money in your hands. You can use it to better your family and win or you can stay the same. My goal is to help you be on the winning team. More than that, I want to show you that you, as the mom, are captain of the winning team. You get to use the knowledge in this book to bring the gold medal home.

Some parts of this book will be encouraging and some will be uncomfortable. I'm going to ask you to examine your habits, to think back to childhood lessons about money, and to wonder about the impact of the culture of money we operate within. I'm going to ask you to consider the hard questions. Why do people handle money so differently? Why are some people so disciplined with money and others aren't? Why are some people so generous and others aren't? How has the history of our culture impacted beliefs about money? What can I do to be an ally to others and to help others improve financially too?

Maybe now you can see why someone with a history background became a financial writer. For me, it's never really been about teaching people how to budget, although that is a part of what I do. It's more about helping people examine their own stories and their past as a way to enlighten them and help them make good choices in the future. It's about helping people face their demons and recognize their own strength to change their money stories. It's about showing moms that they are more than "just" moms, that they hold incredible power. It's about saying I understand. I've been there. Let's grow together.

So, I hope you don't mind that there won't be complicated calculations in this book. Instead, this book is going to be a mixture of personal finance, personal development, some too-personal stories of my own journey with money, and hopefully some encouragement along the way. My goal is to walk with you, inspire you, and help you realize that you already possess all the skills necessary to be a boss with your money. You just have to look within yourself to find the answers, and I'll guide you on that path.

After reading *Mom's Got Money*, my hope is that you'll:

- Understand your money history and your money mindset.
- Effectively manage your money like a boss.
- Work *with* your family in a budget meeting, whether your family is a spouse and several kids or just you and your teenager.
- Ensure that you pay all your bills on time every time.
- Think big when it comes to your future and the legacy you want to leave.

- Surround yourself with friends who will be a positive influence on you, your children, and your financial goals.
- Become an ally to other women and help them succeed on their money journey.
- Learn the art and joy of giving and pass on that lesson to your children.

I will count this book as a success if you connect with just one story in here and it prompts you to take the next step and learn more. My wish is that this book becomes one of many personal finance books on your shelf. The more you read, the more you can craft a personal finance perspective and plan that fits you and your own goals.

Every financial writer has a unique story and personal experiences to bring to the table, and this is likely the only book you'll find by a historian turned financial writer turned mom and entrepreneur. And maybe that's exactly as it should be, because perhaps I'm meeting you at just the right time. You likely need a friend, someone who is a fellow mom and gets it, to help you along the way. And, hopefully, that person is me.

My goal is to help you master a few money lessons so you'll start to truly enjoy money. I would love to help you feel in control of your bills, caught up, and with room to spare. I hope to encourage you to advocate for yourself, improve, and most importantly—breathe.

Eventually, with enough practice, you can become the money boss you were always meant to be, and I'll be right here to help you get there. This is more about mindset than it is about money. And luckily, motherhood has perfectly prepared you to succeed with money. You just didn't know it—until now.

CHAPTER **1**

Shifting to a Boss Mindset

I sat nervously in the waiting room of the student health clinic on my husband's medical school campus. I booked my appointment when my husband had a break between classes so he could be there with me, and I was waiting for him to arrive.

We were there to confirm that I was, in fact, pregnant. Clearly, the five positive pregnancy tests my Type A self took the days prior were not enough for me. I needed answers. Facts.

My husband arrived, and we were led to a small, freezing room where the ultrasound tech was waiting for us. The tech wasn't a man of many words. He hardly greeted us except to tell me to lie down on the cold table so we could start the ultrasound. I shifted nervously, the paper crinkling beneath me, the silence deafening.

There we were, two hopeful (possibly?) new parents, and the tech wasn't speaking as he worked. *Doesn't he want to ask me any questions? Doesn't he at least want to talk about the weather?* I glanced at my husband. He didn't seem to mind the complete silence. He was watching the screen intently, so I thought I should probably do the same.

I looked over at the blobs squinting, trying to make out something, anything. I waited.

It felt like an eternity before tech spoke. Really, it was likely only a few minutes. But, the question he asked tore through the silence like a freight train. His question would change my life forever.

"So, do twins run in your family?"

There's nothing quite like the moment you find out you're going to be a mother. And we all have different experiences, whether we were expecting it or were surprised by it. Maybe you were waiting an exceptionally long time for it to happen or perhaps you waited years to adopt and the phone call finally comes.

In that moment, when the tech showed me my twins, I felt a healthy dose of shock. Much as my husband and I were trying to start a family, I did not once expect to be staring at a screen with *two* little dots on it. That was probably evident from the fact that I said, "Holy shit" over and over and over again, completely unfazed by my husband, who kept whispering, "Shhh, stop saying that!"

I went home that day in a daze, holding the long sheet of ultrasound pictures with little lines pointing to the dots that said, "Twin A" and "Twin B." I cut one of the pictures out and put it in a frame by our bed, and I stared at it. I just couldn't believe it. I felt *different*. I had two extra people with me! The responsibility felt enormous, but from that moment forward, it was clear I had to prepare and plan—after I went and vomited in the trashcan, of course.

One of my core beliefs is that all of us are capable of so much more than we give ourselves credit for. On the day I found out about my twins, I truly didn't know how I was going to manage being a mom to two babies. I was 26 years old with a job, a growing side hustle as a blogger and freelance writer, and a husband who was a second-year medical school student (with such a long, long way to go before he reached the end of his training).

But I knew that, one way or another, I would figure it out. That's the thing; we all have an enormous ability to learn new things and to hone our skills. And, if you're a mom, you already know how to think on your feet. You've already managed incredible levels of responsibility. You know how to plan. And managing your money fits in well with that skill set. Right now, though, you're overwhelmed and you likely don't know where to start. That's why I'm here to help.

For the past decade, I've been supporting other moms in my career as a personal finance writer and financial educator. Through my work and talking to hundreds of other women, I've noticed that money, more than any other topic, produces the most anxiety and emotional baggage. It's also a source of shame and rarely do women feel confident when talking about it.

But, the great thing about personal finance is that the knowledge is available to everyone, and you can build wealth once you find a method that works for you. If you picked up this book, I'm hoping it's because something about the title *Mom's Got Money: A Millennial Mom's Guide to Managing Money Like a Boss* resonated with you.

I want to encourage you by stating I believe anyone can succeed with money no matter who they are, where they come from, or the type of education they have. Some of you have very different starting lines. You may even be the first person in your family to go to college or open an investment account. You may be wading through generations of financial trauma and unfair setbacks. You may be starting with nothing or recently left an abusive relationship. I see you. The best way I can help, as an ally, is to be your guide and have a steadfast belief in your ability to win with money.

I will walk you through the steps to gain financial confidence and take control of your finances. This book is more than teaching you about budgeting or how to raise your credit score. It's about helping you recognize your own abilities as a mom and showing you you're highly capable of making financial decisions.

Right now, you have a lot on your plate. Your family looks to you to make most of the household decisions. Sometimes, the weight of your daily decisions takes a toll. I know it's exhausting to be the glue. But, we have a choice.

We can let this responsibility frustrate us or intimidate us. We can stay up at night worrying if we're making the right decisions for our families. Or, we can step into the role of boss mama with full confidence. Because you see, taking charge doesn't mean being perfect.

It means being powerful, being a planner, delegating, and anticipating that mistakes will happen. It takes leadership, some guts, and a little bit of know-how. And guess what? You have what it takes.

By the end of this book, you'll no longer be a mom who worries about money and her kids' future. You'll be an organized leader who possesses all the skills necessary to run your family ship effectively.

You can have a 9-to-5 job or be a stay-at-home mom or a single mom and still become the boss of your financial life. Stepping into that mindset means you've committed to learning about money, and nothing is going to stop you from improving how your family handles it. It means you have so much fire in you, so much oomph, that nobody—especially not the naysayers—is going to stop you from reaching your goals.

From now on, when you think about your financial journey, I encourage you to consider that you have limitless potential. I want you to think back to when you became a mom, about how much responsibility you took on. If you can do *that*, surely you can handle a little thing like money, right?

But, how can you get there? The best way I can explain it is your brain is incredibly powerful. With it, you have the ability to cultivate a worldview and a mindset that can lead your family and you to a better life. Every single one of us carries within us lessons, triumphs, scars, and failures as they relate to our past, our relationships, and our money. We can use the failures as examples of why we're undeserving of the life we want. We can self-sabotage. We can be overwhelmed. Or, we can decide to do something different.

But, in order to do something different, you have to radically shift your mindset. Your mindset is, to put it simply, your outlook on life. For example, when people discuss having a positive mindset, it usually comes with the glass half-full analogy. But, what many people don't realize is that you can have a friendly, cheerful disposition while simultaneously harboring a negative money mindset, a lack of money confidence, and the weight of intense emotional labor (which I'll explain in full in this chapter).

Let's start with the first one. A negative money mindset, also called a scarcity mindset, shows up silently. It creeps quietly in the moments when you're deciding whether or not to donate to a cause *("I don't have enough money to donate")*. It comes when your child asks to go to camp *("We can't afford that")*. It slips in when your boss tells you to enroll in your retirement plan *("I've always been so bad with money. I don't know how to do that")*.

When you have a negative money mindset, you feel like money is hard. It's confusing. You tell yourself it's too complicated, that you've always been bad with money, and that you can't figure it out. You try to learn about money but you quickly get overwhelmed. You might not want to ask someone for help because you feel like, as an adult and a mother, you should know the answers already. When you have a scarcity mindset, you believe—whether you realize it or not—that you don't have enough. It's hard to part with your money. You're afraid someone's going to come and take it. The worry sometimes keeps you up at night. Negative money mindsets are tricky like that.

Now let's couple that with a concept called emotional labor that's been gaining popularity as it relates to how women feel within their households. In 2017, Gemma Hartley wrote an article for *Harper's Bazaar* entitled "Women Aren't Nags—We're Just Fed Up."[1] This article deeply resonated with women, so much so that Hartley wrote a book on the same topic the following year, *Fed Up: Emotional Labor, Women, and the Way Forward*. Emotional labor, as she describes it, is the mental weight women feel because they manage hundreds of tiny, seemingly insignificant tasks for their households and their children.

Same-sex couples also experience emotional labor. Trish Bendix wrote a response article to Hartley's piece entitled "I Live With a Woman—We're Not Immune to Emotional Labor," which was also published in *Harper's Bazaar*.[2] In it, Bendix explains that same-sex couples can struggle with the same imbalance. For example, if one member of the partnership works from home, she might feel like she has to do more household work. For single moms, emotional labor is amplified. There is no one else to ask at home to help pick up the slack.

These tasks, which take up so much mental space, aren't necessarily put there by partners, spouses, or other family members. They are often the result of cultural norms and how society has evolved. For example, my husband never told me specifically, "Hey, you should be the one to email the twins' teachers, book parent/teacher conference time slots, and RSVP to every birthday party invitation." And yet, I do these things.

Part of it is because I like being involved in my children's schoolwork and lives, but maybe part of it is because I'm doing what I saw my mom do, even though she was a working mom too.

It's interesting that even as moms have entered the workforce in droves over the past few decades, we never quite lost that long to-do list that comes with raising a family. Somehow, we feel responsible for, well, *everything*. For stay-at-home moms, there still remains the cultural pressure to be perfect, to plan dinner, to cater to everyone's needs, and to put yourself last. There's so much silent suffering and pain for someone who means so much to their family.

Have you ever stopped to ask yourself why?

After all, many families have joint responsibilities today and strong partnerships. For example, my husband is a phenomenal cook. He likes going to the grocery store (why, I'll never know.) You can often find him wiping down the counters and loading the dishwasher. He actually *prefers* to be the one putting dirty dishes in rather than taking clean ones out. Please, someone explain that to me.

But emotional labor, as Hartley and Bendix describe it, is more of a *mental* labor. It's the weight of the thousands of daily decisions that have to be made. It's anticipating everyone's needs, especially our children's. It's being one step ahead. It's a brain full of choices, of important dates to remember. It's feeling devoid of energy and conjuring up some more anyway.

It's the constant pressure to squeeze into the idea of what we believe is a *good mom*. And all of this internal chatter is invisible, so no one else knows it's there. How can our families show appreciation or say thank you when it's hard to quantify or see everything that goes on behind the scenes to keep the engine running?

Now, let's take this concept and apply it to money. According to KRC Research, "One in five moms (22%) is a millennial mom, accounting for approximately 9 million people." And guess what? Those 9 million millennial moms "control 85% of household purchases and have a U.S. spending power of $2.4 trillion." Even further, "33% [of millennial moms] are the majority contributor to their household's income (vs. 26% of moms in general).[3] Talk about money power.

And yet, do most millennial moms feel powerful when it comes to money? Do you?

Every occasion you spend time thinking or worrying about paying for school supplies or back to school clothes, you're exercising some emotional labor as it relates to money. One time, I researched for hours to find a "better" backyard playset for my twins because I felt they had outgrown the $200 Walmart version. That was me spending some emotional labor. I even got to scoop some mom guilt on top of the emotional labor when I eventually decided their Walmart playset was fine, and I'd rather save $1,500 than spend it on a nicer cedar playset. I later mentioned it to my husband, and he said he never once thought about the type of playset they had.

That made me wonder if the emotional weight of money decisions goes away once someone becomes incredibly wealthy. Joint research by Vanderbilt University and Regions Bank says perhaps not. Their 2015 Women and Wealth survey specifically targeted private wealth management clients who had estimated household income-producing assets of over $2,000,000. As part of their survey methodology, they said the goal of the study was "to obtain deeper insights into the perceptions and attitudes of Regions affluent customers."[4]

What they found was that "More women than men say they are solely responsible for making financial decisions for their households; however, women express lower levels of financial confidence and optimism than men."

An earlier 2013 study by Allianz Insurance showed some interesting statistics as well. They called it the "Women, Money, and Power Study: Empowered and Underserved." In this study, Allianz surveyed many different types of women from ages 25 to 75 who had household incomes of $30,000 or more per year.[5] They included single women, single mothers, married mothers, divorced women without children, divorced mothers, widows, and those living with partners who were not married.

Among this diverse group, they did unearth some positive findings – namely, 62% of women who responded to the survey had a "strong interest in learning more about finances and retirement planning." Furthermore, 49% of women who responded said that "they have a great deal of responsibility for major financial decisions" and "over half say they are the primary decision-makers."

Yet, even with all this decision making power, lack of money confidence persisted with 49% of women respondents saying they worried about ending up broke and homeless. The study even identified a certain subset of women they dubbed "Women of Influence." Women of Influence have higher incomes than the average woman, are more likely to be successful at work or in business, and are 25% more likely than the average woman to feel financially secure. The study said Women of Influence, who make up about 20% of all women, have more money confidence than the average woman. Yet, a startling 46% of them responded "often" or "sometimes" when asked how often they thought, "Deep down, I worry about becoming a bag lady."[6]

I share this because many women believe if they could just have more money, managing it would be easier. Yet, that's not necessarily the case. Sure, having more money is nice when you're making many, many purchasing decisions for your family. But, both of these studies show that having more money than the average woman doesn't necessarily mean you'll have a dramatic increase in money confidence.

That confidence part—that's what I'm trying to help you improve. That's where my lessons of *managing money like a boss* come in. That research shows more money won't necessarily solve the financial worries women have. So, we have to find another way, a strategy for you to feel content and confident with what you have *right now*, whatever your financial status may be.

So, how do we do that? Well, we know emotional labor is present in women. And, there's also a lack of money confidence, even though women make a significant amount of financial decisions for their families. The lack of confidence can lead to anxiety and worry, which produces money scarcity. The money scarcity is what I referred to earlier in this chapter as a negative money mindset, the worry that you don't have enough or won't have enough one day.

So in order to gain more confidence with money, you first have to combat the negative money mindset that's holding you back from achieving your financial goals. Managing money *like a boss* is about letting go of the typical, overwhelmed mom mindset and taking on the mindset of a confident leader. It's about stepping out of the muck, the difficult stuff, and stepping into your fabulous, mom power.

A boss mindset involves running your household and your financial decisions as if you were the CEO of an organization. And I hear you, it's not easy to feel like a CEO when you're negotiating with a toddler or a teenager (and they're totally winning.) But, that's why our idea of a leader needs to change.

Being a boss doesn't necessarily mean you have all the answers, but it does mean you have the ability to go out and find them or confidently outsource the search to someone else. And, there's no doubt that being a strong leader takes incredible mental strength. You need to motivate your family team, and you'll have to make crucial financial decisions when the outcomes aren't clear yet.

But, I want to make sure you realize that great leaders don't do everything themselves. It might be uncomfortable at first, but part of developing your overall confidence and belief in your own self worth is telling your partner or your kids that you need help. It means becoming a master delegator.

If you're a single mom, it might be uncomfortable at first to enlist the help of others, but it can have a dramatic positive effect on your daily life. Sometimes being strong means directly asking for help. You don't have to suffer to show strength. The more adults you have in your life to trade off help with your children and other duties, the better.

If you have a partner, you might think delegating tasks means more emotional labor for you. After all, isn't delegating going to be exhausting, and why can't they all see that we need help? But, according to a *New York Times* article by Britni de la Cretaz entitled "How to Get Your Partner to Take on More Emotional Labor," communication is key.[7] The article illustrates that it's possible to improve the negative effects of emotional labor, but both partners have to be willing to compromise, check in with each other, and talk about it in a healthy way. If that doesn't work, getting an unbiased, third-party opinion in the form of a relationship therapist can be incredibly helpful.

The goal here is to improve your mindset and how you feel about *yourself* separate from anyone you live with because that will impact how you feel about your decision-making. You're already making a lot of financial decisions, but I'd love for you to feel confident they're the right ones for your family. I want to encourage you to get excited about money, to be curious, and to keep learning.

Remember, as moms, we are already incredibly influential in our families. We shape and mold our children in a way no one else can. But too often, instead of feeling empowered by that reality, we feel exhausted by the weight of our decisions.

In order to transform into a boss mindset, first practice replacing the thoughts of overwhelm with empowering ones. We need to fill our minds with kind and motivating thoughts of what's possible, not ones that make us feel unappreciated and underqualified. This is especially true when it comes to money.

Here are some examples of negative mindset statements as well as examples of boss mindset statements you can use to replace them.

Negative Mindset Statements	Boss Mindset Statements
I can't do this anymore.	I was born to do this.
These kids are driving me crazy.	I can handle this.
I've always been bad with money.	I know I can learn how to handle money.
My culture and upbringing have made me distrustful of money.	I get to learn and decide how I feel about money.
I hate being broke.	I have the power to improve my financial situation.
My parents never taught me about money.	I can learn anything I want about money.
The world is against people like me.	There are allies in the world who will help me.
Why does everyone expect moms to do everything?	Of course they're asking me to do everything. I am the best when I put my mind to something.
I'm so tired.	I'm going to put fresh sheets on my bed and treat myself to an early bedtime.
Managing money is hard.	I do hard things all the time, and once I get the hang of them, they're not that hard anymore.
I'm not good at math.	It's only math. Plus, calculators exist for a reason.

Negative Mindset Statements	Boss Mindset Statements
I have no idea if I'm doing this right.	I'm the mom. I know what's best for my family.
Why doesn't my partner realize I need help?	I'm telling my partner I need help.
I feel so alone as a single mom.	I believe there is strength in asking for help.
Don't they see I'm overwhelmed and drowning?	I'm telling them I'm overwhelmed and need them to step up.
I'm such a bad mom. Why do I yell so much? Why can't I afford that for my kids?	I am a good mom. Full stop.

Ultimately, I believe that all moms have the tools and talents within us to step into that boss role, to realize our greatest potential, and to lead with confidence. We absolutely possess all the intellectual capabilities to tackle hard problems, make difficult financial decisions, and decide what's best for our families. It's just that we've been overwhelmed with our responsibilities and unsure if we're doing things right in a modern world full of opinions and choices.

I know switching negative thoughts to positive thoughts is a lot easier said than done. As I write this book, we're in the middle of the Covid-19 pandemic. Families are suffering. Millions of people are filing for unemployment. Lots of people lost their livelihoods, and many people are getting sick. Moms all over the country found themselves with more tasks to do, teaching their kids at home, while still having numerous other responsibilities. It's been a challenging time for so many people.

I'm quite literally in the trenches with you as I punch the keys on my computer to turn a group of words into a book. Throughout this entire process, my twins have been interrupting me every couple of minutes while I work saying things like, "Hey Mom, guess what? We turned the entire basement into a fort. We used every blanket in the house!"

I never imagined that I'd be writing this book with my kids at home and my husband working at the hospital in a gas mask. Every word in this book was hard-won, hard-fought, and punctuated with words you can't see like, "Please, for the love of God, go in the other room!"

It's funny, though. As challenging as it's been to work and write with the kids in quarantine, something else happened over the last few months: I had to pause. All of us did. We all had to reevaluate our priorities.

Many of you lost jobs and tragically lost family members and friends. An untold amount of you had babies during the pandemic and didn't get to show them off to your family members due to Covid-19 restrictions. All of a sudden, in the haze of the uncertainty, we all clearly understood what mattered most.

It wasn't online sales or salon appointments or extracurricular activities. It was our health, our kids, and our communities. We had to face certain realities and think about what would happen if we lost income for a week, a month, or a year.

I don't know about you, but during the pandemic, I realized a lot of things in my budget that I could "never give up" or "couldn't live without" weren't as necessary as I thought they were. Right now, my budget has the fewest line items it's had in quite some time.

All of us have had to pull strength from places we didn't know existed. We've had to learn how to sit with our thoughts, even the negative ones that are deeply ingrained in our system. We've had the very uncomfortable feeling of not knowing what's to come and if we can keep our kids safe.

We haven't been able to see friends as often or travel, head to the gym or go shopping just for fun. There's been nothing to insulate our feelings or suppress them. This is part of why the pandemic has been so hard for moms, for families, and for the world.

But, the beautiful thing is now you've seen you are very capable of handling something big, something unexpected. You've cared for your family against all odds. You've already led from a place of strength. You've zoomed and homeschooled with the best of them. Truly, moms are the most capable beings on the planet. Will we ever give ourselves enough credit for everything we do? You might not think you've handled hard times well, but you have. You have strength and leadership within you; you're the place your kids call home.

You've proven, especially now, that moms have an incredible capacity to learn and implement change quickly. That takes incredible strength on a daily basis. If you had a minute to really think about it, you'd realize we literally raise and mold and shape *human beings*—even in the middle of things like broken bones, fires, and even pandemics.

Don't you think someone who is capable of all of that, who can weather storms that big, can do something as basic as create a budget and figure out how much life insurance to get? I sure think so. Remember, money is just some numbers on a screen. It's you who gets to give it meaning and tell it where to go. You get to be the boss of it, not the other way around.

With practice and patience, you can step into that boss mom mindset with full confidence. It's already there; you already have it. You just need to give yourself credit for everything you've done and everything you're capable of.

Once you're there mentally and recognize your own power, there's no stopping you. Once you're there, your entire outlook shifts.

And, now that you have some acknowledgment of all the hard things you've endured and many new positive thoughts to practice, it's time to talk about the tools and the strategies that will help you become financially successful.

But, before you start dreaming of your future wealth and all the goals you want to achieve, you have to know where you stand. We'll start by facing the numbers. You can't know where you're going unless you know exactly where you are today.

NOTES

1. Gemma Hartley, "Women Aren't Nags—We're Just Fed Up," *Harper's Bazaar*, September 27, 2017, www.harpersbazaar.com/culture/features/a12063822/emotional-labor-gender-equality/.
2. Trish Bendix, "I Live With a Woman—We're Not Immune to Emotional Labor," *Harper's Bazaar*, October 9, 2017.
3. Weber Shandwick and KRC Research, "Digital Women Influencers: Millennial Moms," www.webershandwick.com/uploads/news/files/Millennial Moms_ExecSummary.pdf.
4. "More Women Than Men Say They Are Solely Responsible For Financial Decisions According to New Regions Bank Study," Regions News Release, October 15, 2015, www.regions.com/-/media/pdfs/Insights-Magazine/PR-WW-Study.pdf?la=en&revision=61bd1595-dfd9-4b5b-a2f2-7cf4f37e44d9&hash=1344F20D317CE5F8B930061C0CEB8202;

"Women and Wealth Study," www.regions.com/Insights/Wealth/hervision-herlegacy/your-life/women-and-wealth-study-2015.

5. "The Allianz Women, Money, and Power® Study: Empowered and Under-served," www.allianzlife.com/-/media/files/allianz/documents/ent_1462_n.pdf.

6. Ibid.

7. Britni de la Cretaz, "How to Get Your Partner to Take on More Emotional Labor," *New York Times*, April 16, 2020 (updated May 8, 2020), www.nytimes.com/article/emotional-labor.html.

CHAPTER **2**

How to Determine Your Household Net Worth

M y husband and I sat at our dining room table after dinner one night staring at two very different spreadsheets we created. The table was a long, old conference table that we bought at an antiques auction. It was big enough to fit several people around it, but there were no dinner plates on it or guests around it that night. Instead, it was filled with stacks of papers that we pored over as we tried to make a huge decision together—the first big one since we walked down the aisle earlier that year.

This was well before we had kids, before we owned our own house, and before I started my business. In other words, we had our entire future ahead of us, and it rested on the decision we made that night.

Each spreadsheet represented a different life path. The documents were full of numbers, calculations, and financial projections trying to predict where we would be financially in 20 years depending on which option we chose.

Spreadsheet A showed what our financial life would look like in 20 years if my husband stayed at his job. We factored in retirement contributions and him getting a modest raise each year. We also calculated in our desire to one day buy a house, have children, and guessed at how much money I'd bring in with my job over time.

We tried to be as conservative as possible when calculating these numbers, low-balling wherever possible. When we were finished, it seemed like if we were responsible with our money and kept investing, we could retire happily and send our kids to college debt-free with the life outlined in Spreadsheet A.

But Spreadsheet B had a very different scenario. It involved my husband leaving the workforce for 10 years to go to medical school and residency training and borrowing hundreds of thousands of dollars to pay for his tuition. In the scenario we created on paper, he would not make retirement contributions while he was in school or in training, even though I would.

We looked up physician salaries in various specialties and put in the lowest one, again trying to be conservative in our calculations. We also added in the time it would take to pay back his medical school loans. We wanted to know if we would be able to meet all our financial goals if we decided to take on that much debt and risk that much lost investing time.

Interestingly, the end results of each spreadsheet were not that much different from one another. One path was predictable with annual raises and a very consistent investing strategy. (That's the power of compound interest and regularly investing in the market.) The other path, the medical school path, had a lot of unknowns and financial risk, but also more potential reward, depending on the specialty he chose in the end. In both cases, though, if things went well, we'd be able to reach our financial goals.

You can probably guess from earlier stories I shared in this book that we—together—chose Spreadsheet B that night. We sent off a deposit to officially make him a part of his medical school class shortly thereafter. It was a joint decision to take on hundreds of thousands of dollars in student loan debt and all the unknowns that came along with it. What's funny is, along the way, I chose my own unknowns, deciding to leave the workforce myself and go full time with my business.

That night, as we went through our calculations, I seriously underestimated my own earning potential. I also underestimated how mentally challenging it would be for both of us to go with Spreadsheet B. And one thing we forgot to calculate was how we would build up substantial savings along the way. We didn't really discuss how we would insulate ourselves if something happened to one of us. We didn't consider what we'd do if one of us developed a medical issue or had a chronically ill child.

Part of that is because we were very young when we sat at the dining room table with our spreadsheets. We were focusing on the hard numbers and not the intangibles. But, I'm so proud of those two young kids for running the numbers before we made a huge financial decision. Even now, the choice we made that night is still the biggest financial decision we've ever made together, more expensive than buying a house or raising kids (thus far). So, it was a good idea for us to take that choice very seriously.

As I write this, my husband is still in fellowship training. He is completing year 10 of 10 of his path to becoming a fully licensed physician. We still have a long way to go when it comes to our financial goals and a significant amount of student loans to pay back, but we're on the way there.

Every month, to keep our financial goals at the top of mind, we do a net worth calculation to see how we're doing financially. A net worth calculation shows us our assets and our liabilities. It's like a temperature reading, showing us how we're doing and reminding us of where we'd like to be.

When you're a boss with your money, you don't go through your financial life blindly. You make a plan and commit to knowing your numbers. Sure, life has a way of being all twisty and turny, and you might not end up where you thought you'd be. But having a plan is a great way to try to get there.

Whatever you pay attention to grows. Whatever you put your focus on magnifies. That's why I'm encouraging you to run your own numbers, to put your own dreams down in spreadsheet form. Nerdy? Yes. Effective? Also yes.

If you've never actually added up how much money you have right now, how many assets you own, and how much debt and liabilities you're responsible before, the time is now. As I mentioned at the end of Chapter 1, you can't move forward with your money journey until you know *exactly* where you're beginning.

So, I'm going to teach you how to calculate your net worth. Knowing this will help you know where you stand, and it will also help you make plans and dream big, just like my husband and I did at our dining room table when we were newlyweds.

Your net worth, not to be confused with self-worth, is quite simply what you own minus what you owe. This is important to know for the purposes of financial goal setting. Your net worth number does not say anything about you as a person. Whether it's way in the negative or impressively positive, your net worth does not define you. It's merely a dot on a graph, a point in time. It's kind of fun to track your net worth, even if you're in the negative because you can see visual progress over time as you achieve your goals. (I realize my idea of fun might be slightly different than most, but humor me here.)

Let's say your goal is to become a millionaire. Some people classify millionaires as people who have $1,000,000 in assets (regardless of their debts). However, my definition of being a millionaire is when you have a $1,000,000 net worth. That's different from having $1,000,000 in cash in the bank. A $1,000,000 net worth means your assets (like cash, a house, and investments) minus any liabilities (like debt) equals $1,000,000. I think this is a more accurate representation of true millionaire status.

Interestingly, with this definition, you can have a million dollars in debt and still have a million-dollar net worth so long as you have at least $2,000,000 worth of assets. Again, that's because your net worth equals your assets minus your liabilities. Wild, right?

So, just because someone has a very high net worth doesn't necessarily mean they're debt-free. It might not even mean they have a lot of cash in the bank.

You might be thinking, "Whoa, Cat, stop with the millionaire talk. I literally live paycheck to paycheck. I know exactly how much money I have. It's the $13 in my checking account!" And to that, I say, what a great place to start tracking your net worth! It's very worthwhile and even more rewarding to start tracking your net worth when you're at the bottom. It makes the graph much more exciting when you reach the top.

Tracking net worth is a very easy exercise to complete, but it's something not a lot of people do. I encourage you to do it, though, because you're becoming a boss with your money, and tracking your net worth is all a part of your mindset shift getting there. Most wealthy people track their money and their investments. If you want to become one of them and join their ranks, this is a simple exercise to complete to get you into that mindset and to set goals of where you want to be.

At this juncture, I want to acknowledge that this net worth calculation will look different for everyone. Not everyone reading this will begin in the same place. That would be impossible. Some of you had to pay for your tuition on your own, using hefty student loans. Some of you are first-generation immigrants trying to create a better life for your families. Many of you watched your parents struggle with money when you were growing up, and that feeling of scarcity leaves its imprint on you. Some of you are on this money journey alone as single moms. Some of you are Black Americans impacted by generations of racism and unfair treatment by financial institutions.

My goal is to be an ally to all of you by sharing my financial knowledge and encouraging you to begin this process. I know that many of you have pain when you talk about money, and that it's deep-rooted. I know that finding out your net worth might be hard the first time. So, to reiterate, my goal is to be a support to every single one of you as a mom and as a financial educator and to help you on this journey. I believe you picked up this book for a reason, and I'm going to try my hardest to ensure it makes a positive impact on your life.

So, with that said, let me give you some examples of different net worth scenarios so you can calculate your own net worth and find out where you stand today.

Net Worth = Assets (What You Own) − Liabilities (What You Owe)

Examples of Assets

- The market value of your house
- Your car
- Cash in your checking account

- Cash in your savings accounts
- The total value of your retirement account(s)
- Any other investment accounts
- Rental properties
- Vacation properties
- Company stock

Some people also include valuables like jewelry and art in their net worth. For me, I only like to include things that are liquidable, things that are cash or could convert to cash with a sale. For example, I'm not going to list my engagement ring in my asset column because it was my great grandma's and I'm not going to sell that. But, you can absolutely list jewelry you have if you'd like to. I'm also not going to list any art I may have because first of all, there are no Picasso paintings in my house. Secondly, the value of my art, furniture, and throw pillows is highly subjective (but I did get a really sweet deal on a Crate & Barrel couch on Facebook Marketplace).

Finding the value of your assets is pretty straightforward. You can look up the amount of money you have in your bank accounts and investment accounts on any given day. You can also look up the value of your cars on Kelley Blue Book. Usually, you'll get the best price on Kelley Blue Book if you select the price for private sale.

If you need to know the value of your house, but you haven't gotten an appraisal lately, you can ask a realtor what they'd list it for if you put it on the market today. Or, you can look up your address on Zillow for a ballpark estimate (although keep in mind that it's just that—an estimate).

Put all these numbers neatly in a spreadsheet and add them up. That's how much you own. Now, let's add up how much you might owe.

Examples of Liabilities
- Credit card debt
- Mortgage loan
- Student loans
- Car loans
- Wedding loans

- Personal loans
- Money owed to friends/family
- Back taxes owed

It's a good exercise to go through and find out the exact amount of your liabilities. If you aren't sure how much debt you have, a good place to start is to pull your credit report. You are entitled to a free credit report every year from each of the three main credit bureaus. Go to www.AnnualCreditReport.com to access it. There, you'll find each and every one of your accounts and debts listed.

On your credit report, you should see the name of your servicer. That's the entity that's in charge of collecting payments for your loans. At the time of this writing, you can also use the National Student Loan Data System (NSLDS) to see your federal student loan balances. The federal student loan system online is reportedly about to undergo a facelift in an effort to make student loan repayments more streamlined. Go to https://studentaid.gov/ for more information.

Once you have all your liabilities in a list, add them up. If you have a lot of them or you've never seen your debts all in a row before, this step might make you cringe or just otherwise hate life. So, I want to remind you that your net worth doesn't equal your self-worth. We're just trying to get a baseline here, a dot on a graph, so that you know exactly where your starting line is. We celebrate all starting dots around here because if you're able to put a dot on a graph, it means you care enough about your money to track it. That is a win in my book.

Next, I'm going to give you a few different examples of net worth scenarios so you can get an idea of what it might look like when you do yours and what you can learn from the information you find.

Scenario #1: Penny

Penny is a single mom to three kids. She's been working as a nurse at a nearby hospital for the last eight years, and the hospital offers many benefits, including a great retirement plan with an employer match. She is still paying off her nursing school loans, but her priority is to get rid of the $4,000 of credit card debt she's accumulated since her divorce. She has a good income and is taking on extra shifts while her mom watches her kids so she can tackle her debt. She is currently renting and wants to know what her net worth is so she can set some financial goals. She hopes to be debt free one day and have enough money to buy a home, fully fund her retirement account, and pay for her kids' college education. Because Penny is trying to meet all these financial goals, she hasn't taken a vacation in quite some time. She does her own nails and shops mostly on resale apps. One day, she'd love to just walk into the mall and buy a whole new wardrobe, but until then, she's working hard to take care of her kids, her patients, and her financial future.

Penny's Net Worth

Assets

Checking Account	$650
Emergency Savings Account	$2,500
Retirement Account	$62,300
Christmas Savings Account	$230
SUV	$6,000
Total Assets:	**$71,680**

Liabilities

Nursing School Loans	$86,000
Credit Card Debt	$4,000
SUV Loan	$8,000
Total Liabilities:	**$98,000**

Penny's Net Worth:
Assets ($71,680) – Liabilities ($98,000) = –$26,320

In this scenario, it would likely take Penny less than an hour to find out her net worth. The benefit of doing that is now, she has a lot of information that will help her move forward with her financial goals. Instead of being afraid to add up her debt, now she knows her numbers, and in a way, she feels relieved.

You'll notice I didn't even say how much Penny makes as a nurse. That's because you don't factor in income into your net worth calculation. Net worth is about how much money you save and invest and how much money you owe to other people. So, it's very possible someone who makes $40,000 a year with a great savings account and no debt could have a higher net worth than someone who makes $100,000 a year, has no savings and $10,000 of credit card debt. In other words, net worth isn't about what you make. It's about what you do with the money that you make.

When I look at Penny's net worth calculation, I actually see a lot of positives even though she's in the negative when it comes to her actual net worth. First of all, she clearly sees the importance of saving. She has an emergency fund and she even has a separate account with Christmas money in it. She's taking advantage of her employer's retirement account, and it's growing and will continue to grow.

Penny now realizes she owes more on her SUV loan than what her vehicle is actually worth. So, if she was thinking about buying a new car sometime soon, calculating her net worth might encourage her to keep the one she's driving a little bit longer. After all, if she buys a new SUV with a loan, not only will she lose money on her current car if she sells it, but it's possible she will add tens of thousands of dollars in a car loan to her liability column, putting her net worth further in the negative.

Taking less than an hour to fill out her net worth sheet could convince her that maybe her SUV isn't that bad after all. Plus, it can help her see the possibility that once she pays off her car loan and credit cards with money from all those extra shifts, she'll only have her nursing school loans left in her liability column. That can make her net worth skyrocket and put her on the path to achieving her goals.

For Penny, I would recommend that she keep working those extra shifts until her credit card and car are paid off. With a lot of dedication and focus, this can happen faster than she thinks. Once those are paid off, I'd recommend she add more money to her emergency fund. With three kids at home, $2,500 isn't enough especially if you deal with more than one financial surprise in a month. Given the unexpected nature of life, a great goal would be to have a six-plus-month emergency fund.

In the past, I've always recommended people have a three- to six-month emergency fund. Now that I'm writing this book during the Covid quarantine, I see the value in having six-plus months in savings just in case. She'll also need a strategy to pay off those nursing school loans. That might mean refinancing them to a lower interest rate and waiting to buy a home until she's much more ready. There's absolutely nothing wrong with renting and allowing your landlord to pay for those big home repairs while you use your money toward your next financial goal. There's no rush when it comes to homeownership. It's a fantastic goal to have, but it's one you want to be fully ready for when the time is right. Also, since Penny has been working hard and going without self-care or a vacation lately, it would be a good idea to create a savings account just for her, similar to her Christmas savings account. She can add money to it every month and then use it for a quick weekend getaway or a mall trip to buy a few new items. If she sets it aside and saves for it, it will help her to not feel guilty about using that money on herself instead of her debt. When it comes to money, there has to be some sense of balance. It's okay to reward yourself with small things, especially if you have a few years before you're able to accomplish all your financial goals.

Now, let's look at another net worth scenario.

Scenario #2: Jazmin and Josh

Jazmin is a 24-year-old newlywed who just found out she's pregnant with her first child. It was a bit of a surprise, but they're extremely happy to be growing their family. Plus, she and her husband, Josh, who both work in marketing, recently bought their first house. The only problem is, when they paid for their down payment, closing costs, and the move, they pretty much drained their checking and savings accounts, which makes them both nervous with a baby on the way. Lately, Jazmin has been wondering if she'll go back to work after her maternity leave. She'd never considered being a stay-at-home mom before, but being pregnant has changed things. She wonders if it's even possible for her to be a stay-at-home mom with the new house payments and lack of savings. So, she and Josh decide to sit down together and complete a household net worth calculation to see where they stand.

Jazmin and Josh's Household Net Worth
Assets

Joint Checking Account	$150
Joint Emergency Savings Account	$300
Jazmin's Retirement Account	$6,000
Josh's Retirement Account	$6,000
Jazmin's Car	$23,000
Josh's Car	$2,000
Josh and Jazmin's House Value	$175,000
Total Assets:	**$212,450**

Liabilities

Jazmin's Student Loans	$14,000
Jazmin's Car Loan	$23,000
Josh's Student Loans	$3,000
Joint Credit Card Debt	$2,000
Mortgage on the House	$120,000
Total Liabilities:	**$162,000**

Jazmin and Josh's Household Net Worth:
Assets ($212,450) – Liabilities ($162,000) = $50,450

When Jazmin and Josh complete their net worth calculation, they'll notice they have a net worth of $50,450. It's a good feeling to have a positive net worth. It doesn't mean they're debt-free, but it does mean they have more assets than liabilities. For Jazmin and Josh, it looks like buying a home was a good investment. Their house is currently worth more than what they owe on it. However, because they recently used all their savings to pay for a down payment and other fees to buy the house, you'll notice that their available cash in checking and savings is very low. They also have student loans and a small amount of credit card debt. But, they're making the right choice by participating in retirement plans. Because they're young, at only 24, they haven't been out of school for very long. So, they don't have a lot in retirement, but it's a good start. It also looks like Josh has a paid-off car, while Jazmin has awhile to go to pay hers off.

When I look at their numbers here and when I think about Jazmin's curiosity about becoming a stay-at-home mom, a couple of things come to mind. First, although they have a positive net worth, a lot of their money is tied up in their house and in their retirement accounts. They need to increase their cash savings before they do anything else. Not having solid cash savings when you are a new homeowner is just asking for problems to happen. So, in this scenario, I'd encourage them to take a few months to stockpile cash both for their home and for their new baby.

Next, when it comes to whether Jazmin can become a stay-at-home mom, that depends on income. As I mentioned previously, income isn't a part of the net worth calculation. Net worth is about what you do with the money you have. Her husband may be a high earner. If so, with some good habits, they might be able to save enough money over the next few months before the baby comes for them to get a better cash position, pay down some of the higher interest debt, and prepare to be a one-income household.

If they don't have high incomes right now (which is likely since they're just starting out in their careers), it's going to be a challenge for Jazmin to be a stay-at-home mom purely based on these numbers. But, there's nothing like a baby to make you reassess your money habits. If staying home is truly something Jazmin wants, she's going to have to become BFFs with her budget. It will take a lot of scaling back, sacrifices, and perhaps even big moves like selling her car to buy something way less expensive, in order to make her goals a reality.

I'd recommend that this couple spend some time looking at their income, their spending, and their childcare options. Knowing these numbers and knowing their habits will help them decide on the best next steps for their family. They should also do some calculations when it comes to their investing and retirement goals. Will Jazmin still be able to contribute to some type of retirement plan, like a spousal IRA, if she chooses to be a stay-at-home mom? If not, will Josh's retirement investments be enough for both of them when the time comes? With a baby on the way, are they going to make sure they have term life insurance in a worst-case scenario? Will Josh's job pay for health insurance for the whole family or will that be an added cost? Will they be able to easily afford their mortgage payment if Jazmin stops working?

As you can see, this young couple has a lot to consider. Too often, moms only weigh the cost of childcare versus their take-home income when deciding whether to stay home with their kids. But, it's important to take a step back and look at the whole picture to make sure you can truly afford it. Jazmin should consider the value of the benefits that make up her total compensation package—things like her retirement contributions, insurance, social security contributions, and more. It's important for her to consider her future self as well as her current self when analyzing the costs and benefits of her choices.

Regardless of what Jazmin and Josh choose for their future, what's important is that they're facing the numbers now. They're taking a deep dive into their finances and they're making a plan for what they want. When you step back and do a full overview when it comes to your money, you can see when things seem out of balance. And, if you sit down and do this exercise with your partner or spouse, you can spend some time talking about long-term goals together.

I realize that not every couple will feel comfortable calculating a joint household net worth. It's possible you want to keep your financial numbers to yourself. That decision is up to you. I personally like doing my net worth calculations jointly, mostly because it's helped my husband and me plan long-term as a unit. It's also built camaraderie going all the way to the day at the dining room table with Spreadsheet A and Spreadsheet B.

But, based on your past experiences, you might feel strongly about having your money completely separate from your other half. If that's the case, I support you in that too. Even if you keep your numbers on different net worth spreadsheets, you can still have a lot of conversations about your goals for the future. Open communication is the goal, whether your numbers are blended together or not.

Scenario #3: Dana and Jimmy

Dana is a 35-year-old yoga instructor. She's built quite a local following, and people love coming to her classes. As soon as she opens up a time slot for a new yoga class, it immediately sells out. She's that good (what a boss)! She enjoys teaching yoga mostly because of the people she meets and the flexibility it brings. She likes being the one to pick up her kids from elementary school at 2:30 each day. Her husband, Jimmy, who is 37, works long hours in construction. He gets paid well, but the construction company he works for doesn't offer much in terms of retirement benefits. However, he is able to work overtime when they need it.

Both Dana and Jimmy work hard and try to give their kids the best life possible, but they both have dreams of more. Dana has always wanted to own her own yoga studio, but she is debt-averse and doesn't want to take out a business loan to get her own space. Jimmy wants to transition to a more supervisory role and earn more money. He wants to be able to pay for his kids to go to college one day.

Both Dana and Jimmy are relatively frugal and good at saving, but they really want to learn more about investing. Up until now, they haven't invested anything because they're afraid they'll lose the money they worked so hard for. But, the more they talk, the more they realize that in order to move forward and have enough money to send their kids to college, they need to start learning more about finance. As a first step, they sit down to complete a net worth calculation together to see where they stand.

Dana and Jimmy's Household Net Worth
Assets

Joint Checking Account	$4,750
Joint Emergency Savings Account	$5,000
General Savings Account	$37,000
Dana and Jimmy's House Value	$140,000
Dana's Car	$9,000
Jimmy's Truck	$7,000
Total Assets:	**$202,750**

Liabilities

Mortgage on the House	$72,000
Total Liabilities:	**$72,000**

Dana and Jimmy's Household Net Worth:
Assets ($202,750) – Liabilities ($72,000) = $130,750

As you can see, Dana and Jimmy have some really excellent financial habits. The only debt they have is the mortgage on their house. They own their cars outright and they've built a considerable savings account. They have a solid emergency fund and an additional savings account for anything else they want to do in life, whether it's updating a bathroom in their home or taking a family vacation. They've been diligent and careful with their money, and it shows.

The next step for them is to begin investing in their own retirement accounts so they can set themselves up for success in the future. Both of them work physically demanding jobs, so it's a good idea to plan for the long term in case they want to comfortably retire in the future.

At 35 and 37 years old, there is still enough time to invest and build up a nice nest egg for their later years. It is important that they start now, though.

If I were them, I would prioritize investing for their own futures over saving for their children's college education right now. There are many ways for their children to pay to go to school, but if they don't want to be a burden to their children when they're elderly, it's better to focus on their nest egg. As their incomes grow over the next decade, they can start thinking about setting up college accounts for their kids. But for now, they need to learn as much as possible about investing long term so they feel more comfortable with the idea of it. With more education, they will realize that although there might be fluctuations in the market, investing for the long term for 20-plus years will generally yield a good return, one that will help them grow their savings far more than having it sit in a savings account.

I think Dana's goal to own her own studio one day is a great idea. Owning a successful business is a very good way to accelerate your net worth growth. I don't think she has to borrow money to start it, which is her primary concern. Instead, she can start slowly by offer-ing classes on her own, whether it's in her backyard or a local park. She can open a business account and set herself up as a legitimate business entity. Once she gets a solid business savings in her account, she can rent a small space for a few months and see how things go. She can ask her students to trade classes for any services they might be able to offer, like logo design, social media marketing, and more. If she uses her network and asks for help from the people who already love her, she could be on her way to building the business she wants— debt-free.

Jimmy might want to look at other work opportunities in the area to find a construction company that does offer retirement benefits to their employees. It would be to his benefit to spend time reaching out to colleagues in the same industry who work at those companies. They can let him know what it's like to work in their jobs and if making a switch might be worthwhile. Investing in work-sponsored retirement accounts is one of the simplest ways to start investing, so that could also be a good way for Jimmy to get started building his wealth for the future.

Scenario #4: Samantha and Christina

Samantha recently moved in with her girlfriend, Christina. They're living in a home that Christina owns, and they both have children from previous marriages. They split their bills but do not share bank accounts. They're trying to find a way to make joint financial goals and save for their kids to go to college all while maintaining their individual accounts. Samantha is 42 years old and works in hospital administration. Christina is 52 years old and works in sales at an art gallery. One day they'd like to retire to the beach, where they can spend their days enjoying the sunshine and entertaining lots of friends and family. But they're not sure if they'll be able to get there financially. So, let's take a look at the numbers. Because they keep their finances separate and Christina is the one who officially owns the house, their net worth calculations are separate.

Christina's Net Worth

Assets

Checking Account	$1,800
Savings Account	$10,000
401k Retirement Account	$110,000
Christina's House Value	$350,000
Christina's Car	$32,000
Christina's RV	$7,000
Total Assets:	**$510,800**

Liabilities

Christina's Car Loan	$14,000
Mortgage on the House	$120,000
Personal Loan	$8,000
Total Liabilities:	**$142,000**

Christina's Net Worth:
Assets ($510,800) – Liabilities ($142,000) = $368,800

Now, let's look at Samantha's numbers.

Samantha's Net Worth

Assets

Checking Account	$4,000
Savings Account	$14,000
401k Retirement Account	$210,000
Samantha's Car	$12,000
Total Assets:	**$240,000**

Liabilities

Samantha's Car Loan	$9,000
Credit Card Debt	$37,000
Total Liabilities:	**$46,000**

Samantha's Net Worth:

Assets ($240,000) – Liabilities ($46,000) = $194,000

So, first I want to say I love the goal of retiring on the beach someday. I think Christina and Samantha should spend some time researching little beach towns and put up pictures of homes they like on an inspiration board. Putting visual reminders all over the house can remind them to stick to their financial goals when they're tempted to veer off. Once they know the price point of their dream beach house, they will have a goal to aim for. They can even make a spreadsheet of how to get there, much like my husband and I did when deciding whether he should go to medical school.

Knowing a little bit of their backstory and that both had been previously married, the credit card debt and the personal loan could be a result of fees incurred during a divorce or when they needed extra money to get back on their feet. Now that they are more settled, it would be a good idea to get rid of any high-interest debt they have. Neither has student loan debt and both have retirement accounts, which is great for their financial health.

I noticed that Christina has an RV. I don't know if they use it a lot or not, but if they don't, she might consider selling it and putting the proceeds of the sale toward her car loan, which will speed up the process of paying it off.

Once Christina and Samantha pay off some debt, they can start to think about their other goal, which is helping pay for their kids' college education. Any money they were spending on credit card payments or car payments could be used to increase their own retirement contributions, pad their savings account, or start college funds.

With the help of an accountant, they can decide on the best college savings accounts to open. Typically, parents open a 529 account or an ESA, which is an Education Savings Account, to save for college. Each option has different max contributions and tax benefits, which is why it's helpful to consult an accountant.

They can also start to map out a plan for their retirement goals, which might mean increasing retirement contributions so they have more to live off of and one day perhaps selling Christina's house and using the proceeds to buy the beach house.

Sometimes working together on money goals, especially after you've been previously married, can seem really stressful. But, one way to alleviate that stress is to talk about goals together and what each person is going to do to contribute to getting there. That discussion can be the beginning of many more money meetings where you can watch your net worth grow, either individually or together, over time.

As you can see, knowing your net worth and using it to see if you can achieve your biggest goals is an important exercise when you're getting your finances in order. There's a reason why I placed this chapter before the budget meeting chapter. It's because you need a broad view of your money and where you stand before you get into the details of your daily spending and bills.

I also like that you can see the direction your money is going when you do a net worth calculation. The goal is to clean up the liability column while you grow your asset column. Due to the wonders of compound interest, investments tend to grow on their own over the long term. But debt, especially high-interest debt, grows too—in the wrong direction. So, the more money you can funnel into the asset column, the better for your long-term financial success.

What's important is that you start where you are, even if your net worth is very much in the negative. Remember, mindset is important here, so even if you're in the negative, I want you to think of how cool and amazing your graph is going to look five years from now.

This is about achieving your biggest life goals and mapping out a plan to help you get there. Sure, there will be bumps in the road along the way, but if you know where you're starting, it will empower you to take the next step.

In the next chapter, I'll teach you how to conduct a family budget meeting. Managing your daily spending is an important part of growing your net worth and reaching those big, audacious boss-mom level goals.

CHAPTER 3

The Family Budget Meeting

T he intercom crackled as the grocery store cashier picked up the receiver to speak into it. My eyes grew wide; it was too late to stop her. Her voice reverberated throughout the store: "Customer needs assistance with a WIC check."

I wished at that moment that the floor would open up and swallow me whole.

I tried to do all the "right" things to prepare for motherhood financially. I used my business income to save a large baby fund. I made sure I had enough freelance writing clients so I could support our family. We lived frugally and saved as much as possible because my husband was a student and I was new to being self-employed.

But, the expense of my twins' NICU bills, a huge cross-country move, and the difficulty of working from home with two newborns meant our savings started to dwindle at a rapid pace.

When our twins needed an expensive, specialty formula, our pediatrician suggested we could get help paying for it by applying for assistance at a WIC (short for the Special Supplemental Nutrition Program for Women, Infants, and Children) office. WIC is a government program that helps low-income mothers and babies get the nutrition they need. If you qualify, you get checks that you can bring to the grocery store to use for formula and food. (Even if you've never used a check yourself, you might have noticed the letters WIC next to certain food on the grocery store shelves.)

Although I was very grateful for the help, the way people treated me when I used them made me feel like a failure. That day, the first time I handed over a WIC check to the cashier to pay, she stared at the checks, confused. She asked me what they were, and I felt my cheeks flush as I explained. Then, she told me that no one ever used those checks at that store and she had no idea how to put them into the computer. That's when she picked up the intercom.

At that point, a dad behind me in line with two young sons got exasperated from having to wait for the manager to come and help. So, he let out a huge sigh, left *all* his groceries behind mine on the belt, and stomped out of the store.

I was standing there with my own two kids, rocking their double stroller back and forth to try to keep them happy while we waited. I'll never forget looking at the back of that dad's head as he dragged his own two kids out of the store, hopping mad that we had delayed him buying his own groceries.

When I eventually, mercifully, checked out and made my way to the car with the formula, both babies were crying. I joined them, tears streaming down my face all the way home.

The weight of the moment seemed to pile on all at once. I already felt like a failure at breastfeeding because I never produced enough for both babies. I was trying to do it all—breastfeeding for a few minutes then pumping to try to increase my supply and then still having to supplement with formula. I felt like I was always attached to the pump, always tending to babies, never being enough for anyone.

I felt like I wasn't able to give either of them enough time individually or enough milk. At the same time, I wasn't able to give my business much time or attention either. Then, due to issues with being preemies, the babies rejected regular formula and developed severe reflux, so we needed to try a type that was double the cost.

So, standing there in the grocery store that day, I was already raw. I was already exhausted. I was already 1,300 miles away from all four of my kids' grandparents and all of our siblings. I was in a brand-new city trying to use the WIC checks to try out this new formula, hoping that it would help, hoping the babies would keep it down.

When the cashier had to use the intercom to get assistance using the WIC checks, I felt like she was announcing to the entire grocery store, "Hey we have a mom here who can't care for her kids. Can we get a manager, please?" And when she said *no one uses those checks here* I felt like she was saying *only people who can afford their own formula shop here.*

Even writing this story six years after it happened makes tears stream down my face remembering what that felt like. But, in many ways, looking back, I'm grateful for that experience in the grocery store. It gave me immense perspective and empathy for new moms. I know firsthand that, sometimes, hard-working people go through difficult times. I also know that you can save a large baby fund, announce it to the entire Internet, and use it so quickly, you need extra help. But you know what? It's perfectly fine to ask for help when you need it. That's what programs like WIC are there for. So, if you need to use it, use it, and I hope if you do, your cashier knows how to put them into the computer.

It took a while, but I eventually found my way, and working on my business got easier the older my twins got. I brought in more clients over time, which allowed me to hire a mother's helper so I could get a little work done uninterrupted during the day. I raised my freelance rates, got more press mentions, and eventually made more lucrative business partnerships.

By the time my twins turned three, I was earning six figures from my business, but I didn't forget how I felt the day that dad left all his groceries on the belt behind me. One of my not-so-secret dreams is to be behind a twin mom in the grocery store checkout line who has piles of diapers and formula in her cart and offer to pay for the whole thing for her. I'm always on the lookout.

Managing household spending and budgeting for items for your kids isn't an easy task for millennial mothers. For many, it's challenging to pay for childcare, housing, and food while also paying down debt from student loans, medical debt, or credit card debt. If you add in a car payment and then an unexpected emergency, that doesn't leave a lot of room for taking a family vacation or doing something nice for yourself. It also doesn't leave a lot of room for investing in your future, which is perhaps the most important money goal of all.

This crunch, this feeling of not being able to get ahead (while *really* wanting to) is all a part of the stress and emotional labor I described in the first chapter of this book.

When you feel like you're living paycheck-to-paycheck, when you want to give your kids things that you can't, when you want to get your nails done but you feel guilty about doing it, that's when you make money decisions from a place of scarcity or lack. It's easy to have a negative money mindset when you're trying to budget and you feel like there's just simply not enough. I get it. I was there that day in the grocery store, and I know how terrible it feels.

But, I learned a good way to get in control of your money is to improve the earning part of your money equation and perhaps more importantly, have regular household budget meetings. While I know a budget meeting sounds about as much fun as a root canal, over time the feeling of having a plan and being in control of your money far outweighs any discomfort you might feel during the meeting itself.

Think about it this way: it's hard to stick to a budget, but it's harder to feel broke all the time. It's hard to force yourself to make dinner at home when you're exhausted instead of ordering out, but it's harder to be in credit card debt. It's hard to save money when all you really want to do is spend it on something fun for your family. But, it's harder to have your A/C unit break and not have the money available to fix it.

It's going to be hard either way, but you get to choose your hard. It's either going to be hard now or hard later. Why not just face it now so you're prepared when you need to be?

In this chapter, I'll give you some structure for how to start a family budget meeting. I'll give you some questions to ask, some tips for it to go smoothly (wine helps too), and how to stay motivated to keep talking about money with your family even if it's stressful, even if you want to give up.

THE FAMILY BUDGET MEETING

Family budget meetings are a good idea regardless of what your family looks like or whether or not you share your life with someone. You can have a family budget meeting as a single mom and include your teenager. You can have one with your fiancé or your boyfriend. Perhaps you're a widow and you're overwhelmed. In that case, you can invite a close friend or a sibling to sit down with you as you make a monthly plan for your money.

It also doesn't matter if you keep your money in a separate account from family members or if you share every dime you make. Family budget meetings are more about goals than they are about the dollars. At least, that's what you, with the boss mindset, should convey at the start of every meeting.

If you've never done this before, holding a family budget meeting might feel awkward. Most people don't think a budget meeting sounds like a good time. Truthfully, it might not be at first, but once you get used to it, you might find you actually look forward to them because they're motivating and bring you together with your family.

To put it another way, if you don't have a family budget meeting, how are you going to solidify your financial goals as a family? How will you set aside a time to discuss how much you want to save for retirement? If you never talk about it, you won't have an idea of where you're heading or where you *want* to head. If you sweep your problems under the rug, they will magnify. If you don't speak your goals, it's possible they might never come to fruition.

Just think of all of your family money questions and concerns like tiny little Lego pieces. Every time you pass up an opportunity to talk about them, it's like they get stuck under the couch. They fester there and grow. Suddenly, one day, you decide to move the couch and realize you have enough Lego pieces to construct an entire Minecraft village.

Don't wait until you can build a Minecraft village. Tackle financial decisions as they come up. Don't hide them under the couch. They never really go away; you've just pushed them out of view.

Using the same Mincecraft Lego analogy (because that seems to be my life lately), what if every time you had a budget meeting, it was like you were carefully building a Lego city? Every meeting, the city gets more detailed. You start to see it come together brick by brick. You start to envision what could be. Instead of the Legos festering and growing under the couch all haphazardly, you instead take charge of them and give them a plan.

One thing that helps is to first establish a joint family goal. What do you hope to accomplish together as a family? What do you want your legacy to be? What do you want your grandchildren to say about you? What are you going to do to ensure you get personal freedom?

Many of us walk around our daily lives thinking we are free. You likely picked out what you wanted for breakfast. Maybe you selected your favorite pair of earrings to go with your outfit. Perhaps you brought your child to an activity you researched and chose. While it's great to have the freedom to make those choices on a daily basis, they're not exactly representative of true personal freedom. When you have overarching, indisputable personal freedom, it means no one else tells you what to do or how to live your life. In order to have that, you have to have financial freedom first.

So, allow yourself to dream about what that might be like. Make big, audacious goals. When you come up with that set of goals, erase them and write down new ones that are *even bigger*. Keep going until you can barely write the goals down because they seem so big, so life-changing. When you do that, when you allow your mind to delve into your true heart's desires, something changes.

Write down every single big goal you have, even if it makes you feel guilty, even if it makes you want to hide your list so no one sees it. Then, have your family members do the same. Talk about why those goals are important and what they mean to you even before you ever pull out a calculator to add up some budget numbers. Don't be afraid to talk about hard things. As a couple or as a family, discuss what's holding you back. What's stopping you, right now, today, from getting there?

Here are some of my own very personal top goals. Keep in mind I write these goals in the *present* tense as though they've already happened. This list is not all true today, but it will be someday. Every time I write these goals down, I take one more step into becoming the boss mom I am meant to be.

Cat's Dream Goals (written in the present tense)

- We are 100% debt free, including our mortgage.
- We fully funded our children's college education.
- We're generous with our children and travel with them often.
- We fly first class everywhere we go.

- Our children know the value of money and understand how to earn it and invest it.
- We donate large portions of our wealth.
- Because of us, the goals we set for our family, and the lessons we teach, our family will be wealthy and generous for generations to come.
- Because of our hard work, financial discipline, and generosity, our family makes the world a better place.

These are goals that, a few years ago, I never would have shared with anyone. You're going to read them and initially, you're going to think some of them just seem like *too much* or *too fancy* or perhaps even *impossible*.

Again, I have to remind you that I have not achieved all of the goals on my personal list yet, but I still write them in the present tense as though I have. I like to write them in the present tense because it feels more concrete, as though the result I want has already happened, like I've already become the boss mom I want to be sometime in the future. Now, I just need to take certain steps to get there.

I'd love for you to do the same thing because it's a really powerful exercise. You can even do this jointly as a family with your kids or partner if you have one. My husband and I each have our own goal list, but about half of them are the same. They're things we want for our kids and future grandkids and life together.

So, go ahead and write down your goals. Write them in the present tense, as if they are true right now. Remember, there's the person who you are today and the boss mama you want to become. A great way to start stepping into her shoes is to think and talk as though you already are her.

Think about what future you would say and do on a daily basis. Use your goal list as your guide. This step alone can help you to make dozens of positive financial decisions on a daily basis. Suddenly, instead of worrying about spending $5 on coffee, your focus shifts to the overall impact you want to have on your family tree. The little expenses aren't nearly as important as going for your biggest goals.

I'm not saying it will be easy to create an entire new legacy that will carry on for generations, but the time will pass anyway, so we might as well try. If anything, it's good to move the needle forward, to show your kids that it's possible to improve the position you're in right at this very moment.

I look at my list of goals often. I let them seep into my mind, into my fibers. These goals are a big reason that I don't feel much of a need to keep up with the Joneses. It's why I'm not really tempted to buy products on online ads or why I could care less what the other moms in the school pickup line are driving. It's not because I have superhuman strength or discipline to avoid those things. It's because I have the list! I have goals and dreams for my family, things that are far more important than day-to-day temptations. There is no Earthly want in my life that is bigger or more impactful than the list I just shared with you.

If you can spend time with your family and talk about what you want for your future, that is quite possibly the best way for a budget meeting to start. I realize that these are huge conversations that will require both quiet contemplation and group discussion. So, don't be surprised if your goals list takes a couple of different conversations to create. In fact, talking about your biggest, most audacious life and financial goals shouldn't be a one-time conversation that kicks off your monthly budget series. It should be at the forefront of your mind, something you discuss regularly, something that nudges you and pulls at you when you're trying to make other financial decisions.

Once you do the hard work of creating a list like this, suddenly all your decisions become quite straightforward. The reason is, you can ask yourself, "Does this decision/purchase/idea/trip fit in with my legacy goals? Will making this choice or spending this money help me to get there?" And, if the answer is no, well then, the list made the choice for you. If you've always struggled with spending discipline, this is the most straightforward way I know of to improve it.

You can even write your biggest goal on a sticky note and wrap it around the debit card or credit card you use most. If you're out shopping and you have a big cart full of things you don't need, having to pull off a sticky note that says "Buy a House" so you can buy the clothes in your cart is going to make an impact on you. Again, money is more about your mind than the numbers. It's about knowing your triggers and finding clever ways to beat yourself at your own game.

Now that you have your goals at the forefront of your mind, it's time to create your actual budget with spending categories. If you completed the net worth exercise in Chapter 2, you already have some practice with facing your numbers. But now, instead of looking at the big picture like you did with your net worth, it's time to zoom in. It means taking a hard look at your day-to-day spending over the past few months before you create your budget.

When it comes to some spending categories, you'll be proud of yourself. Maybe you're amazing at scoring deals or perhaps, unlike me, you're a master of meal planning and it shows in your low grocery spending. But, when you get to other numbers, your tendency will be to judge yourself and feel badly about past financial choices.

Instead of getting caught up on what you wish you would have done differently the past few months (or years), I want to encourage you to celebrate the fact that you're taking the time to go over the numbers now. I want you to feel empowered and to remind yourself of all the other hard things you've done in your life.

Remember, budgeting is a skill like anything else. You'd never expect to be perfectly fluent in a language the first month you start learning it. Similarly, you can't expect to be a master budgeter and have incredible discipline right when you get started on this budgeting journey. So, give yourself a little bit of grace and go back to the first chapter if you need a little help on how to replace some of the negative thoughts surrounding money with ones that are more empowering and strong.

Remember that a good leader faces challenges head-on even if they're painful. Someone who is strong sees a problem and decides to work toward a solution, even if it means a complete change of direction or a massive mindset shift.

Most importantly, you raise humans. You can do a budget. I can promise you that.

Here's how to start. First, review last month's spending. This is easiest if you use a debit card or a credit card for your transactions. You can use budgeting software to keep track of your spending and see where most of your money goes, or a good, old-fashioned pen and paper works great too.

The purpose of reviewing your previous month's transactions is to take notice of your spending tendencies and patterns. You might be surprised to learn that your fast food spending is much higher than you expected. Or, you might realize that most of your purchases come from one store late at night.

It's great to notice this so you can be aware of your own habits and start to change them for the better. Remember, this part of the budget meeting isn't to feel shame or beat yourself up about buying things last month. It's simply to make you aware of your tendencies so that if you want to reach one of your money goals faster, you know where to start making small tweaks to get there.

Comb through your prior month's spending to see where your money went and complete these three steps:

1. Write down all your bills and responsibilities.
2. Write down what you expect your monthly income to be and when you get paid.
3. Write down your current debts.

The next step is to create a list of spending categories to incorporate into your budget. Here is a list of some common budget categories in no particular order. Your budget may have more than this or less, depending on what comes up when you review your numbers:

- Mortgage/Rent
- Home maintenance
- Childcare (daycare, babysitter, after school care)
- Children's college fund
- Water
- Electricity
- Natural gas
- Cable/Internet/Streaming services
- Cell phone bill
- Car payment
- Car maintenance

- Gas
- Pets
- Groceries
- Restaurants
- Student loan payment
- Credit card payment
- Personal care
- Gifts
- Clothing
- Household items
- Homeowners insurance
- Car insurance
- Term life insurance
- Health insurance
- Healthcare
- Entertainment
- Giving
- Savings
- Investing

Once you've customized your budget categories to your own needs, write down your take-home income, the exact amount that gets deposited into your checking account.

It's good to base your budget on your take-home income rather than your gross income. Your gross income is the amount of money your employer agreed to pay you. But, if you've ever taken a peek at your paycheck, you know that lots of expenses get deducted from your gross income before your paycheck hits your checking account. These deductions might include retirement contributions, health insurance, and taxes. So, it's important to know your net income because that's the real numbers you have to work with when it comes to your budget categories.

If you're self-employed, as I am, it's even more important to know your net income. Self-employed people are often responsible for making quarterly tax payments, providing their own healthcare, and saving for retirement on their own. You have to know how much you have left over after all of that to truly know how much of your income you have to allocate to your personal bills.

If you have a variable income, whether you're self-employed, working part-time, receiving an hourly wage, or working a commission-based job, it's still possible to budget for your monthly expenses. It took a while for me to do this myself, but in a variable income situation, a great goal is to build a savings account to draw from to give yourself even monthly payments. If you have an incredible month, take a portion of that and save it for the months that aren't as profitable. The more consistent you can make your monthly income, the better you'll be able to budget and get into the habit of managing your money like a boss.

Once you know all your expenses and bills and you know exactly how much money you have coming in every month, it's time to put those numbers together. Take your income and divide it among all the categories you have listed.

So, take a piece of your net income and put it next to your rent/mortgage category. Take another piece and put it in the grocery category. And, keep going until you've allocated your income to all your bills and expenses.

When you do this two things can happen:

1. You have some money left over after allocating your income to your expenses.
2. You don't have enough income to cover your expenses.

If you have money left over after allocating your income to expenses, you are in a great situation. This means you have money left over to save for your future. In this situation, I'm a big advocate for having a plan for any leftover money. Don't just take it as a lump sum and put it in a savings account without knowing what it's for. Instead, be very intentional about where you want your savings to go.

So, perhaps you decide to increase your retirement contributions. Or, maybe you open up a high-yield savings account and make that your holiday spending account. Maybe you set it aside in a car fund so that when it's time to purchase your next vehicle perhaps you're able to do it in cash and live life without a car loan. Either way, start to get obsessed with planning. Dream big and make it a game. Every dollar you're able to save means funding a future goal.

If you've just created your first budget and you *don't* have enough income to cover your expenses, please know that you're not alone. This is extremely common, especially for people who are budgeting for the very first time. Most people decide to start budgeting because they are living paycheck-to-paycheck or because they feel like they can't get ahead. So, it makes sense that if you would put all your numbers on a page you might not have enough to cover everything with room to spare.

But, fear not. This is the beginning of the rest of your financial life. This is the moment you decide to make a change and begin a new habit. Ultimately, there are two ways to solve this money problem and the stress of living a paycheck-to-paycheck lifestyle. You can spend less or you can earn more. I'll talk more about this and freeing up cash flow in the next chapter.

The last part of budgeting I want to mention, before giving you a sample budget, is sinking funds. In a perfect world, your budget will go just as planned without any surprise expenses or issues throughout the month. But, as you know, we don't live in a perfect world. There's going to be something that breaks, whether it's your kid's arm because they fell out of a tree or your hot water heater because it's more than 10 years old. There's also going to be that last-minute birthday invitation that you weren't expecting or a flat tire because you drove through a construction site on your way to work. That, unfortunately, is the reality of life.

In order to prevent these unexpected events from derailing your entire budgeting plan or ruining your day, consider implementing something called sinking funds.

Sinking funds are savings dedicated to things you need to save for over time or use for unexpected expenses. I keep my sinking funds in a separate savings account but some people like to withdraw them as cash and keep them in cash envelopes.

Your sinking funds can include financial goals like a Christmas fund, a car repair fund, a birthday party fund, vacation fund, or anything else you want to save for. Every month, you put the sinking funds as line items in your budget. You save them every month until inevitably, you'll need them. So, if you have an older car, you might want to put $100–$200 in a sinking fund for car repairs every single month. Then, when something breaks, instead of putting a car repair on your credit card, you simply go to your sinking fund and transfer the money into your account or use the cash you've saved in a cash envelope.

You might wonder where you'll get an extra $100–$200 a month to start sinking funds, but don't forget all the lessons you've already learned about spending awareness. Over time, you can make this happen if you continue to work on developing budgeting as a skill and keep track of what you spend. This will inevitably help you find money you didn't even know you had just by simply adjusting some of your daily financial habits.

Having sinking funds has saved me many, many times from completely ruining my budget. My favorite sinking fund is my Christmas fund. I save all year long for Christmas so that when we get to the holiday season, I don't feel stressed. I have everything I need to purchase the gifts I want to buy as well as be generous to others.

I also love saving for vacations ahead of time. There's no better feeling than traveling somewhere with my family knowing I won't have a surprise credit card bill I regret when I get home.

The first time I used a vacation sinking fund was on my babymoon with my husband. We didn't do anything elaborate. We just took a road trip and stayed at a hotel for the weekend. But, I remember we allocated money to go to the movies together. I sat very happily in a big, plush chair in the movie theater with my pregnant belly, buttered popcorn, and candy, not feeling one bit guilty about buying overpriced movie theater food. That's the gift of a sinking fund. It gives you a bit of mental peace and lets you actually enjoy your life, guilt-free.

Here's an example of what a family budget might look like when it has sinking funds as categories.

The Smith Family Sample Budget

Income #1: $3,500/month
Income #2: $2,500/month
Total Monthly *Net* Income: $6,000/month

The Smith Family includes two parents and two kids. They are proud homeowners. Like many millennials, they have credit card debt, student loan debt, car loans, and more. But, they've also worked hard to protect their family by paying for term life insurance and building an emergency fund. They're fortunate to have work benefits that include retirement contributions and health insurance. So, this budget represents how they allocate their total monthly net income of $6,000/month.

Mortgage Payment	$1,200
Electric Bill	$150
Other House Utilities	$50
Streaming Services	$20
Cell Phone Plan	$100
Water Bill	$80
Cable/Internet	$100
Groceries	$600
Gas for Cars	$100
Car Insurance	$200
Term Life Insurance	$100
Home Supplies	$50
Clothing	$50
Gifts	$50
Donations/Giving	$100
Student Loan Payment	$300
Credit Card Minimum Payment 1	$150
Credit Card Minimum Payment 2	$200
Car Payment 1	$400
Car Payment 2	$350
Child's Swim Class	$100
Child's Gymnastics Class	$100

Personal Care	$60
Dining Out	$60
Medical Bills (RX, co-pays, therapy, etc.)	$100
Adult Allowance Fun Money #1	$50
Adult Allowance Fun Money #2	$50
SINKING FUND—Emergency Savings	$100
SINKING FUND—Christmas Spending	$100
SINKING FUND—Birthdays	$50
SINKING FUND—Family Vacation	$100
SINKING FUND—Property Taxes	$300
SINKING FUND—Car Repairs	$150
Total Budget Cost:	**$5,670**

Income ($6,000) – Total Budget ($5,670) = $330 Remaining

In this sample budget, the Smith family set up sinking funds to prepare for both expected and unexpected events in the future. Every month, they add to their emergency savings, Christmas savings fund, birthday, and family vacation fund. They're also saving ahead of time for a big property tax bill so the bill doesn't catch them by surprise and drain their accounts when it comes. Like many millennial families, they also have their children in different extracurricular activities.

Since they have over $300/month extra each month provided they are able to keep their spending within the confines of this budget, I'd recommend they take that $330 and use it to pay off their high-interest credit card debt. Once they accomplish that, I'd recommend they pay off their cars. Paying off those loans completely would free up more than $1,000 a month. Think of what big financial goals they could hit with that type of money available to them. They could save for their kids' college education, go on an extra family trip, or open an investment account to save for their future outside of work-sponsored retirement accounts.

Not only that, but freeing up money in the budget and saving extra for an emergency would insulate them in case one parent loses their job or has a medical issue.

According to the Social Security Administration, the national average wage index for 2018 was $52,145.[1] This measures the amount of money individual people earn from jobs (vs. investment income). The average *household* income had a median of $68,703 in 2019, according to the United States Census Bureau.[2]

So, your household income may be more or less than the Smith family. Either way, try not to get caught up in the details of what the Smith family does with their money. Instead, use this as an example of how to write out a budget. There are no two budgets that will be alike. Families have different priorities, different spending goals, different job benefits, and different incomes. Use your own numbers in your budget and plan and adjust accordingly.

I know many of you read the Smith Family budget and thought things like, "I'd never be able to have a mortgage payment that low in New York/California/etc." or "Why is their grocery spending so high?" or "Why is their grocery spending so low?" So again, try not to worry too much about the Smiths and instead use their template to create your own monthly spending plan.

If you have debt, especially credit card debt, use budget meetings to make a plan for how you're going to pay it off quickly. Take a hard look at your spending and see what you can change so you can allocate as much money as possible to destroying it.

When it comes to paying off your credit card debt, you have to have some passion. You have to start to *hate* your credit card debt because every single day, the bank charges you interest and tries to steal your dreams for the future. On average, your credit card interest rate can be anywhere from 15% to nearly 21% depending on the type of card you have, and that's just the average as reported in October 2020.[3] So, anytime you aren't able to pay your balance in full, you get charged that huge amount of interest. Anytime you're late, there is usually an interest rate penalty, meaning it goes up.

In order to break free from your credit card debt, the first step is to stop using your credit cards. Don't close your accounts, because that can negatively affect your credit score, but for sure cut them up into tiny pieces and say goodbye. That doesn't mean you can't learn to be a responsible credit card user someday in the future, but while you're crushing debt, they're too tempting to keep around.

In some cases you may be able to do a credit card balance transfer where you move your credit card balance to another credit card that has a 0% introductory rate for a period of time. Then you can make more headway when you make payments because all your payment will go toward the principal, not interest.

Sometimes, though, a balance transfer is not possible, especially if you have a lower credit score. It can even slow down your process and make you feel lax because you're not accruing interest during the introductory rate offer period. Plus, there's usually a fee to transfer a balance, like 3% or 5% of your balance, which can be pretty high depending on how much credit card debt you have. Ultimately, moving debt around might feel like progress, but you'll only make a true dent in it when you start paying more than the minimums—hopefully a lot more!

Once you finish paying off your credit cards and you're ready to tackle your other debts, use what I call the Debt Incineration Method (thanks to my Instagram community for helping me name it!) With this method, the next debt you pay off is the one that makes you the most angry or the most ashamed. There are plenty of debt repayment methods, like the Snowball Method and the Avalanche Method, but I like my Debt Incineration Method because it prioritizes your mental health.

I know there are some debts you have that make you feel ashamed. Maybe it's a student loan from a college you dropped out of. Or maybe it's a loan for a car you deeply regret buying. It could be a debt to a family member, an old personal loan you took out to go on a trip with an ex-boyfriend, or something else. If there's a debt in there that makes you cringe every single time you think about it, get rid of that one first. I believe our emotions are powerful and our mental health is the most important aspect of any wealth-building journey.

So, don't leave the debt you hate the most until last just because of the interest rate or the amount. Incinerate it first. Stop letting it torture you. Tell it that you are the boss, not it.

In order to incinerate debt, do whatever you can. Get your family involved. Purge your basement. Deliver food. Take on a weekend side job. Go crazy on it until it's gone. You won't have to work every weekend or evening forever, just until you pay it off.

Debt will kill those dreams and goals you wrote down. High-interest debt especially makes it so hard to climb out of a debt hole. I would love for you to be striding toward investments and reading more and more money books, not contemplating bankruptcy and looking up phone numbers for bankruptcy attorneys. You can do this. You've been focused before. You've been fierce before. You can make your kid stop doing something with just one look and no words. You're a powerful mama. So, use some of that power on your debt.

If this is motivating for you, good. That zest and excitement early in your budgeting journey is necessary for you to have a great start. But, if you start noticing that your enthusiasm wanes after a few months, you're not alone.

Maybe you get tired of sticking to a budget. Perhaps you don't see as much progress as you want to see month after month. Or, if you're budgeting with a partner, maybe trying to budget together creates a lot of stress and arguments.

Every time this happens, every time you want to give up, look back at that big list of goals I asked you to create earlier in this chapter. Those goals, your whys, have to be more powerful than any minor daily want. You have to keep going back to your list of goals and keep reminding yourself what's at stake. Your desire to achieve whatever you want for your family has to be more powerful than any Instagram ad trying to make you buy new clothes.

What I want out of my own financial journey, what I want for my family, what I want to create for many generations after me, is more powerful than anything else. It's greater than any temporary want. That is how I stay motivated and unconcerned with what other people are driving or wearing.

I don't count how many moms in the school pickup line are carrying designer handbags or get into cars newer and fancier than mine.

None of that is more important than the big, audacious goals I have for my family, the ones I (with much trepidation) shared with you. There is no material possession and no fancy dinner out that is better than my long-term goals. And, if you don't have something like that, something so powerful and so big that it drives you to be better every day, then I encourage you to take some time to think about it. Dig into those goals on your list and find one that speaks to you and moves you in a way nothing else has.

Put the list of goals somewhere you can see it regularly. Look at the goals every day to help you stay focused. Only when you have these ideas in place can you start to manage your spending, pay off debt, earn more, and build a life others can only dream of. When things get really hard, it's those thoughts and beliefs that you can fall back on.

If you feel discouraged, I want you to know, I get it and that's normal. The entire process seems incredibly overwhelming. But, you'd be surprised at how much progress you can make in just a short amount of time. The key is to get started, to take control, and not to let anyone (not even the rude guy behind you in the grocery store line) make you feel like you don't deserve a brighter future.

If you need to have little treats along the way to keep you motivated like booking a weekend trip once you've paid off all your credit card debt or booking a facial when you get a raise at work, that's fine. But, the longer you stay committed with your eyes on the prize, the greater the reward when you finally achieve the goals on your list.

If you experience conflict during a budget meeting with your other half, that's normal too. Once, my husband and I had an argument about how much he spent on hair products. (Yes, him, not me.) Admittedly, he has absolutely gorgeous, swoopy McDreamy type of hair. But, come on! We laugh about it now, but early in our journey of budgeting together, we had to learn how to work together. That involved him thinking more about his purchases, but it also involved me learning how to not micromanage him, which I admit, isn't an easy feat.

Stressful conversations, or outright arguments, with your partner might make you not want to have budget meetings again. But, if you keep trying and keep working toward your goals together, I think you'll find you'll start having more successful meetings than stressful ones.

Some tips for keeping budget meetings productive and civil when you're having one with someone else include:

- Allowing each person to talk and share their opinions without being interrupted. (Is it just me or is getting interrupted *the worst?*)
- Starting the meeting by going over your goals, especially your joint goals, so you remind each other you're on the same team.

■ Considering implementing an allowance policy, where each person gets a certain amount of money they can spend each month, no questions asked. We did this after "the hair incident" and it's made us a lot happier. (I share more details about this in the next chapter.)

For the record, my husband and I still disagree about money sometimes. But these days, we have a lot more respect for each other's purchases and far less judgment. After years of budgeting together, we trust each other's opinions and know we're on the same team. But it's taken years for us to get there and tons of open conversations about money to get comfortable talking about it.

Whether you budget with someone or not, I encourage you to keep working at it. Get an accountability partner if you're a single mom. Implement those sinking funds and see how great it feels to slowly fill them up over time. I want to emphasize that budgeting is not something I'm trying to encourage you to do to make your life harder. I'm not trying to prevent you from buying the things you like.

Rather, I'm trying to gift you the tools to create incredible peace of mind. With practice, you'll learn how to spend money on the things you love and eliminate the rest. Remember, the goal is to get clear on your goals and free up cash flow so you can pay off debt, save, and invest in your future. That will help you to create real, true wealth for your family and children.

In the next chapter, I'll discuss exactly how to free up cash flow and improve your budget, especially when your expenses are more than your income. I'll also share my favorite budgeting technique for giving yourself great peace of mind. At the end of the day, that's what I want to give you—mental peace when it comes to money. So, let's keep going.

NOTES

1. National Average Wage Index, Social Security Administration, www.ssa.gov/OACT/COLA/AWI.html.
2. Jessica Smega, Melissa Kollar, Emily A. Shrider, and John Creamer, "Income and Poverty in the United States: 2019," Report P60-270, U.S. Census Bureau, www.census.gov/library/publications/2020/demo/p60-270.html.
3. Joe Resendiz, "Average Credit Card Interest Rates (APR)—October 2020," ValuePenguin, www.valuepenguin.com/average-credit-card-interest-rates.

CHAPTER 4

How to Manage Your Household Cash Flow and Start Saving

"I can find you a house with more bathrooms if you raise your budget by about $20,000 more," our real estate agent told us. She explained, "It will likely only increase your monthly payment by a bit. Can you come up at all in your budget?"

I could, but I wouldn't.

We were living in New Jersey but searching for a three-bedroom, two-bathroom house in Michigan, where my husband matched into a residency program.

We made the 10-hour drive from New Jersey to Michigan twice to go house hunting with both two-year-olds in the car. So, you can imagine how crazy the process was—it was not like you see on HGTV!

Although we wanted a three-bedroom, two-bathroom house because we'd all been sharing a bathroom since the twins were born, those houses seemed to be out of our price range or snapped up quickly overnight.

I never dreamed the Detroit metro market would be so hot, but it was. Every house we looked at had multiple offers on it. We lost the first house we decided to make an offer on to an all-cash buyer. And, these were all small bungalows, what some would call starter homes. Most of the houses in our budget had one bathroom, not two, and I quickly realized I would have to compromise on what I wanted if I was going to stay under budget.

When my real estate agent asked me if we could raise our budget by $20,000, she was trying to help us. As a busy mother herself of young kids, she knew buying a home with one bathroom would be inconvenient for us. She also knew that if we could raise our budget by a little bit, it would open up several new houses to tour that we hadn't considered yet. But, here's the thing: I wasn't in a rush to have a "dream home" or exactly what I wanted. I'm still not. I wanted to buy what I could very easily afford with plenty of room to spare.

When we found our home, I didn't love it at first. The layout wasn't something I would have picked, and it was showing its age, as it was built in the 1950s. But, it had a big backyard for our kids and dog. The kitchen was updated with granite countertops, and it definitely had potential. My husband told me that we could save up to finish the basement to add some square footage and that we could eventually upgrade our appliances to stainless steel. The bones were good, and despite the fact that all four of us would be sharing a bathroom, I knew we could make it work.

We decided to put an offer on the house, but four other people had the same idea. Again, we couldn't believe how many people were trying to buy a house in the same area. I remember our real estate agent called us shocked when the buyer chose us. "I can't believe it, but you got the house!" she exclaimed.

Part of why we got the house was that we were very flexible with the buyer. We allowed her to rent it back from us for 60 days, which greatly complicated our own schedule. However, in the end, it enabled us to be the ones to get the keys. I also wrote her a nice note with my offer with an adorable picture of my family telling her how it would be our first home and how much our pup would enjoy her very first fenced-in backyard.

Having lived in our 1950s bungalow for over four years now, I can say with confidence that it was the right choice for us. I don't mind that it's a bit small because of the peace and freedom our low mortgage payment brings us.

I've never once worried about not being able to make my mortgage payment because I simply didn't buy a house that was a stretch for me. After all, being a business owner means I have a variable income, and I have to be cognizant of that. When we bought the house, my husband was still in training, and I was still in the early stages of full-time business ownership. We bought a house that was appropriate for us at the time. We weren't trying to pretend we were wealthier or further along on our financial journey than we actually were.

Most financial experts recommend you buy a home with a payment that's around 25–30% of your monthly take-home pay. I agree that's a reasonable percentage, especially if you have a large emergency fund. But, I took an even more conservative route. Our house payment is less than 15% of our monthly take-home pay.

That came in handy when our property taxes went up the first year of owning our home. It also helped when our hot water heater needed replacing to the tune of $1,600. Then, my husband said he wanted to do one extra year of training after he graduated from residency. The catch was he'd have lower pay for that year, and the fellowship program he wanted to do was in the next state over. That meant he needed to rent an apartment for a year and come home on the weekends. The only reason he was able to take that opportunity and pay for an apartment without worrying was because we bought a house we could afford on one income.

Right now, there is a lot of pressure on millennials to buy their dream home right away. Society is very good at convincing people they "deserve" the very best. Many families tend to upgrade to bigger and better homes throughout their lifetimes. Rarely do people stay put like my 96-year-old great uncle who's lived in his house for over 60 years. (It still has the same furniture and pink carpet that it did decades ago, and he takes excellent care of it.)

When we were looking for houses, I thought about my great uncle, who raised six boys in his modest house. I also thought about my husband, who grew up in a small house that belonged to his grandmother, and their family of six all shared a bathroom until my husband was in the seventh grade. Then, they moved into the home my in-laws still live in today, one they built over the course of several years and paid for in cash despite having a modest income. My great uncle and my in-laws knew what it meant to delay gratification, to wait, and it has served them well.

My own parents bought an old fishing camp not long after I was born and renovated it. When I was in the eighth grade, they added on to the house. They didn't do it all at once. They waited years until the time was right. So, I know that in the future, I can upgrade my home if I want to. I had no illusions that I had to purchase the biggest, most beautiful house on the block as my first home. There's a huge advantage to waiting until you're financially ready for the next step.

And, for the record, there's nothing wrong with wanting a big, beautiful home. Put it on your dream board and go for it! I'm emphasizing that many young people want perfect, Pinterest-worthy houses right away when they're just getting started in life. I would never expect my first home to be like my in-laws' or my parents' house, because they worked 20–30 years to get to that point. If I tried to be at their level now, before I'm financially ready, it could put me in significant financial hardship. Instead, I'd rather enjoy the journey along the way and see where it takes me.

The difference between how older generations grew up and today is millennials experience a barrage of billions of dollars of marketing dollars designed to make us buy. No longer is advertising limited to newspapers or commercials. I can't pump gas or walk through the grocery store without being assaulted with an ad on a blinking screen. I can't even browse a pair of $50 shoes online without a website reassuring me that I can break up the purchase into "three easy payments."

The problem with this is that millennials can afford just about anything these days if it's broken up into enough monthly payments. And the more payments you have, even if they're really tiny, the more it disrupts your cash flow. There's a common refrain that "cash is king," and I'd like to rephrase that to "cash flow is king."

Paying attention to cash flow is one of the most important skills you can master when becoming a boss with your money. Cash flow is the money you have flowing in and out of your bank account every month.

What you want is more money flowing in than out. So yes, I could have purchased a slightly more expensive house with an extra bathroom, but that would have meant more cash leaving my bank account every month. And, I don't want my cash to leave. I want it to stay, because then I can use it to save, invest, and grow my wealth.

When it comes to cash flow, there are three main expenses that can make or break your budget. I call them the three anchors.

The Three Cash Flow Anchors

1. Your house
2. Your car
3. Your food

When it comes to buying a home, it's very important to know that banks base the amount of home you can afford on your gross income, not your net income. We've already established that your gross income is your income before any benefits or retirement contributions get taken out of your paycheck. Banks also look at the amount of debt you have (so they can calculate something called a Debt-to-Income—DTI—ratio) and your credit score. What they don't know is how many vacations you like to take a year. They also don't know that you spend money taking care of your mom or that your daughter is a competitive gymnast (and gymnastics costs you $500 a month).

Only you know your real monthly cash flow numbers, and only you should be the one to say what house you can afford. Just because a bank is willing to give you a big mortgage loan doesn't mean you should take it.

Too much house means too much cash flow going out. You have to decide what your priorities are in your life and how homeownership fits into that. You don't want too much of a house payment to take away the ability to go on a family vacation or pay for your child's extracurriculars.

While I'm on the topic of homeownership, I also want to say there's absolutely nothing wrong with renting. The American Dream really pushes people to feel like they aren't successful unless they actually own a home. However, buying and selling houses is an expensive process. Ideally, you should save 20% down on a home to avoid paying something called private mortgage insurance (PMI), which is an extra bill you have to pay if you put down less than 20%. Private mortgage insurance provides no real benefit to you; it's intended to protect the bank if you default. Additionally, PMI can sometimes come at a high monthly cost, although certain types of mortgage loans, like VA loans, will waive PMI if you put down less than 20%. Home maintenance is also expensive, especially if you have little kids who find joy in seeing just how much maintenance they can create for you.

You will never hear me say that owning a home is essential to building wealth. It's certainly one way to grow your assets in that net worth column, but it's not the only way to do it. Many people choose home-ownership using the argument that in their area, having a mortgage payment is cheaper than their rent payment. And, while that may be true on paper, make sure you fully understand that the house payment you're comparing is likely less than renting because you will put thousands of dollars down on a home first.

Additionally, you will likely have to pay thousands of dollars to close and ideally have thousands of dollars in savings for maintenance. Oh, and don't forget random things like the $400 sidewalk tax bill we unexpectedly received one week before Christmas just a few months after we bought our home.

Yes, homes do typically appreciate in value, so they're nice to have in the asset column of your net worth spreadsheet. But, it's important to run all the numbers, as homeownership might be more expensive than you realize. In fact, according to a 2019 survey, 63% of millennial homeowners expressed regrets about their home purchase, citing unexpected costs as the biggest issue they encountered.[1]

When you own your home, sure you can paint the walls any color you want, but all repairs will come out of your bank account. When you rent, you usually have a set monthly payment, and your landlord is responsible for repairs. There are pros and cons to both, and when you decide which is right for you, make sure you consider your available cash flow as part of it. It might seem like renting costs more when looking at monthly payments, but it's likely that it's less overall when you factor in home-buying costs, maintenance, and general upkeep.

Don't be afraid to downgrade into a more affordable home to improve your cash flow or pursue other financial goals. Similarly, don't let society convince you that you need to be in a rush to buy a home. When my best friend got pregnant with her first child, everyone assumed she would buy her first house (you know, because the world expects you to check all their made-up boxes if you're going to be a mom!). Several people were very surprised when my friend said that she had no intention of buying a house until they were ready. She was perfectly content with bringing her baby home to her apartment.

I reminded her that I lived in a house that was converted to two apartments for the first two years of my twins' lives. I walked up and down a flight of stairs every day carrying both car seats, and our downstairs apartment neighbors often complained once the twins learned to walk and started running around upstairs. It was the right choice for us at the time, though, and no one should dictate how you spend your money or raise your children. Can I get an amen?

The next budget anchor when considering cash flow is cars. According to data from Experian Automotive, the average car payment for a new car as of Q1 in 2019 is $554, and for a used car it's $391.[2] Plus, now you can get a car loan for eight years! In the past, five years was more commonplace as the loan term when financing a car. According to Experian's data, the amount of car loans between 85 and 96 months used to finance new cars increased 38% in Q1 2019.[3]

The problem with having car loans of that length is depreciation. According to a study that analyzed over 7.7 million used and new cars, on average, a car's value will depreciate almost 50% over the first five years of ownership.[4] Because of that, if you have a long car loan term coupled with a high interest rate, you can see how very quickly, you can owe much more on your car than what it's worth.

Of course, dealerships aren't worried about your cash flow or your personal pursuit of wealth. They will happily let you trade in a car, even if you owe more on it than it's worth. They'll roll that difference, called negative equity, into a new car loan for you. Unfortunately, that means you drive off the lot with a huge new loan and monthly payment on a car you still owe more on than it's worth. Once you start that cycle of rolling negative equity into new car loans, it can be extremely difficult to get out of it.

If you want to make a change with your car and lower your car payment, consider this. You can always buy a nicer car one day once you get to a better financial position. Your car is just a car. Society has made it a status symbol and a sign of success. For most people, though, it simply represents a big loan and a big car payment every month. Don't let the car illusion funded by other people's debt make you feel like you, too, have to have the newest, nicest car on the block.

I'm not saying you have to drive a car that's falling apart or breaking down every mile. You're a mom and many of you are driving little kids around. I know you want something reliable and safe. I also realize that while you're new on your financial journey, many of you might find it difficult to buy a car in cash, at least initially. So, start by downsizing.

Here's an example. If you currently own a newer car with a $500 monthly payment, sell it and buy a reliable, normal $10,000 used car. If you take out a 60-month loan (not an 84- or a 96-month loan) for this vehicle at a 4% interest rate, your monthly payment would be $184 per month. That immediately frees up $316 of cash flow every month, money you get to keep. You can use that to pay off debt or put it in a sinking fund for car maintenance so getting new tires won't break your entire budget. You could also set it aside and save up to buy your next car in cash because the only thing better than lowering your car note is not having one at all.

Your kids are going to put crushed goldfish on the floor of your car whether you drive a used Honda Accord or a new BMW, so you might as well purchase a car you can easily afford. Your car says nothing about you as a person, and anyone who treats you differently based on what you drive isn't worth your time and doesn't have your best interests at heart.

Interestingly, researchers found that while it may seem like driving a luxury car would make you happier, it rarely makes a difference once you get used to driving it day to day. We all like things that are shiny and new because they're fun and exciting. But, once you are sitting in traffic and your focus is not on the newest tech features in your car, the car itself no longer produces the same level of happiness.[5] In sum, the study concluded, "The car matters when the car is on the driver's mind, but not otherwise."

Most of us are driving, dropping kids off, and trying to merge into traffic at the same time kids are asking the same question for the seventh time. I don't think many of us have a moment to sit and marvel at how nice the steering wheel is in a luxury vehicle.

As I said, there can always be a time and place for driving expensive cars in the future. Until then, there are many safe, affordable options you can buy that can get you from Point A to Point B, all while improving your cash flow substantially.

If you currently lease a car, I'd encourage you to consider shifting to owning a car once your lease is up or trying to find someone to take over your lease. Even though I know monthly payments on a lease are low and the cars are new and nicer, you never actually own your car with a lease. You never gain it as an asset. You can never pay it off; it belongs to someone else. You can't sell it or put it in the asset column on your net worth spreadsheet because it does not belong to you. You're borrowing something shiny that looks nice to other people and then you eventually have to turn it back in. You'll always have a monthly payment to make with a lease. You can't ever delete it from your budget spreadsheet and free up that cash flow because you can't pay it off because it's not yours. For those reasons and more, I'm an advocate for buying a car over leasing one.

The third and final anchor in any budget is food. I really struggle in this category because I don't enjoy cooking. The good news is this is the easiest category of the three anchors to improve quickly. Selling your car takes some time and mental effort. Finding a house you like within a reasonable budget can also take time and be a mental drain. But food? That's something you can improve today.

I'm not going to spend a lot of time on this category because I think it's pretty self-explanatory. Plus, I get really tired of a lot of personal finance advice geared toward moms that *only* talks about saving money at the grocery store, using coupons, and shopping around for the best deals on your Sunday roast (as if that's all we're capable of doing to get ahead financially).

Because I think moms are incredibly smart and savvy, I'm going to give you a lot more credit than that. If you want to save money at the grocery store, I trust you can log onto Pinterest and find dozens of affordable recipes. If you want to use coupons or shop your grocery store sales fliers, I trust you can do your research and figure that out too.

Really, what this category comes down to is planning and discipline. I find that it's better to allow yourself some ordering out and restaurant trips rather than try to cut it out completely. We all need a break every now and then, and I'm the last person to try to tell you to stop buying food out.

What's helped me is allowing myself to order food every Saturday night. Ever since the pandemic started, we've begun a family movie night tradition. My kids are allowed to sleep on an air mattress in our room, and they get so excited. We usually order a pizza and sprinkle M&Ms on our movie popcorn to make it extra special.

My goal is to try not to order out or hit a drive-through during the week to keep my restaurant/takeout spending in check. I know throughout the week that movie night is coming, so even when I'm tired during the week, I try to rustle up something for dinner at home, even if it's simple. This "rule" of ordering out only once a week keeps my food spending in check while also allowing me to be human and give myself a break every now and then.

Over the past few years, I've done plenty of experiments where I've spent a month only using food from my pantry or have tried to only spend $50/week on food (it involves a lot of soup!). I've also had months where I've spent an astonishing amount on food when my husband and I did rounds of the Whole30 program or stocked our basement with some items at the beginning of the Covid-19 quarantine. I think it's good to know what type of food you can make when you want to save money so you can always dial down your food spending during a tough month. Trying different spending challenges and putting your focus on cutting food spending, even if it's just for a month or two, can help show you what's possible and just how much cash flow you can free up if necessary with just this one category.

Ultimately, when you review your spending on the three anchors and make changes in even one of these three categories, you can dramatically improve your cash flow to the point where you won't have to feel guilty about an occasional small purchase like an Amazon dress or a Starbucks cake pop. The more you go after the big payments, the more you increase your cash flow. The more cash you have, the more opportunity you have to actually grow your wealth.

This isn't free rein to go wild on the small purchases because it's important to watch those too. But, if your sole goal is to free up cash in your life, look to the three anchors first. Then go about improving habits on your smaller purchases.

If you're feeling some resistance when it comes to improving the three anchors, take a minute and remember your big goals. If you free up cash flow, you can pursue other financial goals, like saving for your kids' college and your own retirement. Find a goal that's bigger than you, one that gets you fired up, one that helps you make those hard choices now so you can have a much better life in the future.

Once you get into a new groove and become someone who has more cash flow, you'll notice you're thinking about money a lot more—in a positive way. Perhaps you spot new opportunities to make money or find yourself returning items you've been meaning to return for days so you can get a refund. Maybe you're reading more about investing and you start to read stories of others who win with money. Eventually, you'll become someone who is aware of their money on a daily basis.

The next step to improving cash flow is to get one month ahead. I know this seems like a big ask, but bear with me for just a moment so I can explain why I manage my money in this way. Hint: it has to do with saving brain space.

One month ahead budgeting means that you have all of the money you need for the month in your checking account on the first of the month. Then, as the month goes on, you pay all of your bills as usual. I prefer to pay my bills automatically so I just keep tabs on them throughout the month to make sure the correct amount comes out.

While money flows out of your bank account to pay your bills, it also flows in when you get paid. So, if you're disciplined and stick to your budget, you should start the next month with everything that you need on the first of the month again.

You can do this even if you have separate accounts from your partner or if you're single. If you have separate accounts from your partner, I recommend assigning bills to each person so your partner might be responsible for the electric bill and the daycare bill and you might be responsible for the water bill and your rent or mortgage. If you split bills down the middle, you can set up a system where one of you sends the other half of specific payments.

I have tried just about every budgeting system there is, and I've found that automating my bills and being one month ahead is the most stress-free way to budget imaginable. That's why I'm recommending it to you because as a mom, you have enough on your plate. You don't need a system that requires a ton of time and upkeep. When you're one month ahead, your only job is to make sure you have all the money you need for the month on the first of the month. If you can do that and automate your bills, you don't have to worry whether you have enough money in your account to pay them. You don't have to worry about overdrafting, and you don't have to worry that checks will bounce or your cards will get declined.

How many times during the month do you worry about a bill that you have to pay but you don't have enough money to pay it? Or, how many times do you have the money to pay a bill but you completely forget to pay it because you're so busy? Perhaps you remember but then notice it's a bank holiday, which might make a payment late. When you budget one month ahead and automate all your bills, it really eliminates all the stress associated with making money and paying your bills.

Now you might be wondering how in the world you get one month ahead. If you're not used to being one month ahead, it might feel impossible. You might be thinking that it sure sounds really nice, but never would something like that be possible for you. It takes a bit of discipline and patience, but I want to encourage you to try.

First, complete the exercise outlined in Chapter 3, where you know all of your expenses and your income in great detail. You have to do this because you have to learn what number you need to start the month with in your bank account. If your bills and debt payments equal $4,000 a month, you will need $4,000 in your bank account on the first of the month in order to fully embrace this type of budgeting.

It might take you some time to reach this goal. I know that $4,000 won't fall out the sky so you can start next month budgeting one month ahead. However, you can sell some high-ticket items, you can cut back on ordering takeout this month, or you can try your hand at a side hustle with the goal of getting one month ahead. Doing this a few months in a row can enable you to slowly but surely build up your account enough to where you start the month with all the money you need for that month.

When you're trying to shift your bills to a one-month-ahead system, remember the acronym ROADSS.

Here's what it stands for:

R: Research past spending and bills

O: Omit unnecessary expenses

A: Ask for discounts for services and insurance

D: Determine how much money you spend each month

S: Sell everything in sight

S: Side hustle temporarily

Here's a little bit more detail about each step.

R: RESEARCH PAST SPENDING AND BILLS

As I've mentioned a few times in this chapter, the most important piece of information you need is how much money you spend on your bills and expenses every single month. Comb through the past two to three months of your spending and organize them into categories. If you primarily spent cash without logging your expenses, this can be a little challenging to do. But, if you use a debit card or a credit card for the majority of your expenses, you should be able to pull your last couple of statements and see how much you spend each month. If you prefer to use cash, keep detailed records of your spending for two months to help you understand how much cash actually leaves your hands.

O: OMIT UNNECESSARY EXPENSES

When you go through your past spending, you are going to come across some cringeworthy purchases. You're going to see exactly where your weak points are and where you're doing the majority of your spending. If you start recording your cash spending, you might notice you're much less likely to actually use your money. That's because tracking your spending actually brings a lot of awareness to your habits. If you find that you'd like to spend less, go ahead and omit unnecessary expenses. This will help you to reach your one-month-ahead goal that much faster.

A: ASK FOR DISCOUNTS FOR SERVICES AND INSURANCE

Now you can take some time to make phone calls about the services that you pay for including insurance. Pick up the phone and speak with your cable company and your car insurance company. Ask them if you qualify for any discounts or if there's anything else they can do for you. If you pay for things like having someone cut your grass or shovel your snow or landscape, consider taking on at least one of these tasks yourself to save money on that expense. Remember, we don't have to do this forever or give up the things you like forever. We're just trying to reach the goal of getting one month ahead and that might mean temporarily giving up a gym membership or calling customer service at a few different companies in order to free up some cash.

D: DETERMINE HOW MUCH MONEY YOU SPEND EACH MONTH

Once you've negotiated down your bills and have more awareness about your spending habits each month, you should have a more exact number of the amount of money you need every single month in order to be able to automate all your bills with ease. This is your goal number, the number you want to see in your bank account on the first of every month.

S: SELL EVERYTHING IN SIGHT

In order to make your goal of getting one month ahead a reality, it's time to sell everything in sight. Get down in your basement and let things go. Have a garage sale. Post a huge children's clothing purge on Facebook Marketplace or in one of your mom groups. Will it be a lot of work? You bet. Is it worth it so you can get one month ahead? Absolutely.

S: SIDE HUSTLE TEMPORARILY

The last thing you can do if you still need a boost to get one month ahead is to side hustle temporarily. This isn't something you have to do forever, but side hustling for a couple of months can give you the necessary funds you need to start the first of the month with all the money you need for the month.

So, there you have it: ROADSS can help you make this financial shift.

The last thing I'll say about getting one month ahead is that doing this is a gift to yourself. It's hard work to start managing your money this way, but it can give you great peace of mind. I don't know about you, but with all the worry and anxiety that comes with being a mother, it's really helpful to know that whether or not I can pay my bills isn't among them.

I know it's hard to conceive of having all the money in your account for a whole month, but I would argue that it's harder to worry about money every day and not know if you have enough to pay your bills. I know it's hard to think about automating your bills, especially if you're someone who regularly pays bills late and it gives you anxiety to think about the money automatically going out. But, I would argue that it's harder to go every single month of your life worrying about not having enough. The idea of getting one month ahead is nothing new. It's not something I created. It's something many people do across the world because it offers great peace of mind.

And, because I am writing to help moms especially, I want you to know that I know you have a lot on your plate. I know that you have many responsibilities. And I know that while your partner falls asleep instantly at night next to you, the worries about your kids and your day and money often keep you up at night. But, there is one thing you don't have to worry about and that's your monthly bills if you can learn how to get one month ahead.

Ultimately, it takes time to improve your cash flow and develop the habit of monitoring your money. Budgeting takes work. Being mindful of cash flow takes practice. You won't be good at it right away, and that's perfectly okay. This is not something that magically changes overnight.

If you wanted to run a marathon, you probably wouldn't wake up tomorrow, put on your running shoes, and run 26.2 miles right away. Rather, you'd take it slow, training a little bit at a time. You'd run more each day and get better at it each day. You'd make a choice to eat less bad food and instead choose food that energizes your body to run. Eventually, over the course of a few months, you'd likely reach your goal because you worked toward achieving it inch by inch, even when you wanted to quit, even when it seemed hard.

The same is true for budgeting and money management. It's entirely possible you will hold a budget meeting next month and you won't see much change. What's important now is that you make small decisions every day to improve your financial situation.

So, start with paying attention to your three anchors and getting one month ahead. In the next chapter, I'm going to teach you how FICO calculates credit scores and what you can do to raise yours. A high credit score can help you refinance high-interest debt, which can also free up cash flow, so it's an important part of taking the next step toward financial freedom.

NOTES

1. Deborah Kearns, "Nearly Two-Thirds of Millennial Homeowners Have Regrets about Their Purchase, Survey Finds," Bankrate, February 28, 2019, www.bankrate.com/mortgages/homebuyers-survey-february-2019/.

2. Matt Tatham, "Auto Loan Debt Sets Record Highs," Experian, July 18, 2019, www.experian.com/blogs/ask-experian/research/auto-loan-debt-study/.

3. Ibid.

4. Julie Blackley, "Cars That Hold Their Value," iSeeCars, www.iseecars.com/cars-that-hold-their-value-study.

5. Norbert Schwarz and Jing Xu, "Why Don't We Learn from Poor Choices? The Consistency of Expectation, Choice, and Memory Clouds the Lessons of Experience," *Journal of Consumer Psychology* 21, no. 2 (2011): 142–145, dornsife.usc.edu/assets/sites/780/docs/11_jcp_schwarz___xu_why_we_don_t_learn__fin_.pdf.

CHAPTER **5**

How to Increase and Maintain Your Credit Score (and Why It's Important)

I am having my life screwed over by a Nordstrom credit card.

That's the message my friend Alex (not her real name) sent me, asking for help. Alex is a very cool single mom to two girls, and she's usually diligent with her money. For example, she bought her car with cash, she owns her own business, and she's great at finding beautiful clothes for great prices.

But, caught up in all the stress during the Covid-19 quarantine, she completely forgot to pay her credit card bill, the first time in the history of having that card that it happened. Because of this one late payment, her FICO credit score dropped 81 points.

She said, "I spent the morning in tears wondering how I could have one late payment and it can drop that much. I don't know what to do."

Alex was, in her own words, completely pissed at herself. I hated to see my friend upset, so I tried to get to the root of what was bothering her. "Are you trying to buy a new house soon? Is that why you're worried that your score took a hit?" I asked. "No," she replied. "Well, then why are you beating yourself up about this so much?" I asked. After all, I knew if she just gave it a little time to recover, her score could bounce back.

But for Alex, the frustration went much deeper than that. She explained that when she was younger, she wasn't educated about money and she made some mistakes. Since then, she's worked extremely hard to learn about managing money and increase her credit score. She took pride in paying attention to her finances. Then, when she got divorced, she had to rebuild her life as a single mom, and having a high credit score was important to her. To her, it was a sign of independence. It meant that she was financially secure and didn't need anyone else to help her finance big purchases in the future.

So when her credit score dropped 81 points in one day, it didn't just make her angry. It rocked her sense of security. And it's that panicked feeling that can contribute to a scarce money mindset.

I reassured Alex that her credit score meant nothing about her as a person. This is not *The Scarlet Letter*. We don't have to go around wearing sweaters with our credit scores on them for everyone to see. Plus, being late on a payment is a mistake that a lot of people have made, myself included.

I knew if she made all her payments on time again consistently over a period of a few months, her credit score would eventually go back up. This one late payment would not have to define her for years.

That reassured her, and sure enough, only three months later, her score jumped 35 points, and it continues to go up. We agreed that perhaps she should take a break from checking her credit score every day. It was causing her stress and became an obsession. Instead, it's best to check it about once a month just to see how you're doing.

Also, before I get into this chapter on credit scores, first let me say that I view credit cards and credit scores as a bit of a necessary evil. I don't love credit cards. I think they cause a lot of damage and heartache in families, and I personally lose a lot of my spending discipline when I use them. I do own credit cards, but I don't use them regularly. I use my debit card and my one-month-ahead budgeting system for just about every single purchase I make. However, I do put one expense a month on a credit card, like my Netflix bill, so the credit bureaus see I'm using a card and paying it off regularly. I've successfully disputed purchases with my bank connected to my debit card, so I do have access to fraud protection like you would with a credit card.

Plenty of my friends who work in the same industry as I do use credit cards every day, earn airline miles, and have solid arguments for why they think credit cards are better for day-to-day spending. But for me, it comes down to personal preference and knowing myself. I simply have more discipline when I know money comes directly out of my checking account, with no credit card "runway" to save me or give me time to come up with the money to pay for what I just bought. It keeps me organized and disciplined, which is a great way to manage money.

You should know that it is entirely possible for you to go through life without debt, without a credit card, and without a credit score. And, if that's what you want to do, you don't need to read this chapter. Debt does not have to be a fact of life like many people think. You can still buy a house with a mortgage company that does manual underwriting for a mortgage. You can still pay for a car in cash. You can also rent a car with a debit card through some companies. But, more and more often, companies that provide services, like car insurance companies, are using your credit score in their applications process. Those with excellent credit scores typically get the best rates. That's why I call credit cards a necessary evil and why I still have them. I know having a high credit score is very useful in some situations and guarantees me very competitive interest rates that will save me money over the course of my lifetime. I monitor my credit and keep track of my credit score, not obsessively, but enough to know what's going on. The truth is, credit scores are a measure of how you handle debt or the credit extended to you. It's important to use that responsibility wisely and to know where you stand.

If you're wondering how to check your credit score or how the numbers are even calculated, you're in the right place. After reading this chapter, you'll be a knowledgeable boss mama, capable of making your own decisions about your use of credit. You'll learn exactly how the choices you make could affect your credit, which will help you to get on track and stay on track when it comes to your money.

So, let's start with the most important thing: your credit score is *just a number*. It's kind of like how math is *just math*. And budgets are *just budgets*. The credit score you have attached to your name says exactly *nothing* about the type of person you are. You're not a bad mom if you have a low credit score. You're not uneducated or *bad with money* or a loser or whatever you tell yourself if you have zero clue how credit scores work (or how you got the one you currently have).

As you'll see below, credit scores can be a little confusing. The world of credit reports is highly complex, and to make things even more difficult, there's not just *one* credit score attached to your name. There are several. But my goal is not to overwhelm you. Once you have the basics down and you know how it works and how to improve your score, it's game on.

We're not going to be able to predict with exact precision that if you do x, you'll get exactly an 800 credit score. But, what I can do is share a few things you can do to raise your score and then keep it that way.

If it helps, you can think of a credit score like a grade. The class you're in is called Financial Choices, and if you make a lot of right choices, you get an A. As I said, this grade has no reflection on who you are as a person. Your credit score doesn't know about that casserole you baked for your friend who just had a baby or how you volunteer at a soup kitchen every other Friday. All it knows is a simple list of loans and transactions. It's a financial record, and for better or for worse, that record comes with a grade—a score.

The records are held with three main credit bureaus: Experian, TransUnion, and Equifax. These three agencies maintain all your credit information and put it all together in what we know as a credit report.

Another company—the most well known being the Fair Isaac Corporation or FICO—then takes that information and assigns your credit score. If the information on your credit report is positive, your score will likely be good. If you have a few, but not a ton of blips on there, you might have an average score. If you have lots of late payments and bills in collections, you might have a poor credit score.

FICO isn't the only type of credit score. There are other credit scores like a VantageScore and even the recently released UltraFICO™ score (which considers your checking account records). But, for the purposes of this chapter, we're learning about what affects FICO scores because that is the credit score lenders most commonly use when deciding whether to offer you a loan.

Also, here's the good news about credit scores: if you have a low credit score, you can raise it. You won't be stuck with your grade forever. In the school of life when it comes to your finances, you get a lot of chances.

Your credit report should have a list of every credit line you have, how much you owe, and whether or not your account is in good standing. When you look at your report, you should see a list of the credit cards you have, your student loans, as well as your car loan and mortgage if you have those.

Sometimes the three credit bureaus have the same data. Other times, the data might vary. This shouldn't be too concerning unless the data on your report is flat out wrong. That's when you need to contact the credit bureaus to get it corrected. Most of the time your credit report shows the past seven years of your financial life. You should see every time you've paid a bill on time. If you missed a payment and were more than 30 days late, you'll see that on there too. If you have an account in collections, it'll be listed near the top in the adverse accounts section.

But remember, even if your credit report has some blips or issues on it, that doesn't say anything about you as a person, as a mother, or as a human being. It's *just* a credit report. It's simply a record of your financial habits that you can change and improve upon over time.

Credit scores usually range from 300 to 850. So, you might be wondering, "What's a good number?" And when do we need to say, "Hey Mama, let's work on this"?

Credit Score	Rating	What It Means
300–579	Poor Credit Score	It might take lenders time to trust you. It will be very difficult to get credit. If you need to borrow money, you'll likely have to pay deposits, fees, or crazy-high interest rates.
580–669	Fair Credit Score	This is a subprime credit score. You might be able to get credit with this score, but interest rates will be high. You might be able to get a secured credit card to rebuild your credit. Buying a home is sometimes possible with this score, but I don't recommend it.
670–739	Good Credit Score	When you have a good credit score, you can typically apply for home loans and other forms of credit. While you won't get the absolute best interest rates, you're on the right track.
740–799	Very Good Credit Score	Go ahead and dance, Mama. Your very good credit score shows you've made smart financial decisions, and you pay your bills on time. Lenders will likely offer you excellent interest rates if you have this score.
800–850	Exceptional Credit Score	Okay, now you're just showing off. With this score, you should be able to get the absolute best interest rates available and get approved for credit cards that have sweet perks.

Much like the Google algorithm or the Instagram algorithm, the exact way FICO calculates your credit score is a bit of a secret. But, the good news is they don't leave us completely in the dark. They've provided a rough formula—a general overview if you will—of the factors that make up a credit score and how much they weigh into it, which you can see in the following chart.

Payment History	35% of your credit score
Debt Owed	30% of your credit score
Length of Credit	15% of your credit score
New Credit	10% of your credit score
Diversity of Credit	10% of your credit score

As you can see, payment history is the biggest slice of the credit score pie. If there's anything you take from this chapter, take this: paying your bills on time, every time, is one of the best ways to earn and maintain a good credit score.

Think about it: If someone asked you to borrow money, but you had a piece of paper telling you that they were late on half their payments, would you want to lend them money? Nope. The banks feel the same way about customers who want to borrow money but have lots of negative marks in the payment history category. A little judgmental, I know. But, it's a reality nonetheless.

The amount of debt you owe in relation to the amount of credit you have makes up 30% of your credit score. This is also called credit utilization, that is, how much of your available credit you're currently using.

What credit utilization really shows is how much restraint and discipline you have when it comes to your money. If you have a credit card with a $5,000 limit, do you have a $0 balance, a $2,750 balance, or is it totally maxed out with no room to spare?

The gold standard (and the way to financial freedom) is to pay off your credit card in full each month. But, if you're just getting started paying down your debt and raising your credit score, a good first goal to have is to get the credit utilization of each of your cards down to 30% of your total available credit. So, if you have $5,000 of available credit on your card, try to get your balance below $1,500. This, in the eyes of creditors, shows that you have some restraint, the ability not to use *all* of the credit offered to you.

Oh, and for some reason, someone started this terrible rumor that in order to have a good credit score, you have to *keep* a balance of 30% of your total credit on your card. To quote Gwen Stefani, that is B-A-N-A-N-A-S. Keeping a balance on your card and paying interest to the credit card companies is never the way to financial success.

The goal, as I said, is to first get your credit utilization under 30% on each card. Then, the prize-winning goal is to pay those babies off in full.

The part of your credit score that measures the length of your credit history is pretty straightforward and makes up 15% of your score. Having a credit file for a few years gives you a slight edge over someone who just got their first credit card. For many people, the first type of debt they incur is student loans. If you've never had a loan before, like a car loan or a personal loan, your student loans might begin your credit file, even if you don't have an actual credit card.

If you want to get a credit card but you've never had one or you currently have a poor credit score, you have some options. You can apply for a secured credit card. With a secured credit card, you give your creditor a deposit. That deposit becomes your credit limit. When you spend on the card and pay your bill on time, the creditor reports positive news to the credit bureaus. If you can't pay your bill, the creditor can use your deposit so they won't have a loss.

You can also apply for a basic, starter credit card. I got my first beginner credit card when I was 21 years old, and it had a $500 limit. I did have a credit file because of my student loans, but I had a low income (my graduate school assistantship paid only $12,330 per year!). Because I handled that credit card responsibly, I was able to get approved for other credit cards down the road with higher limits and more perks.

Next up is New Credit, which makes up 10% of your score. This part of your score indicates how many times you've pursued new credit or how many times lenders have made a request for your credit score or credit report to see if you're an eligible borrower. According to FICO, credit inquiries stay on your report for two years, but they only factor the last 12 months of inquiries into your credit score.

The reason inquiries matter is because if you have a lot of them, it could indicate that you're in financial trouble and looking for more ways to borrow money. Sometimes people worry that if they shop around for rates, like for a mortgage or an auto loan, this will reflect poorly on this part of the credit score. However, FICO is smart and the algorithm can recognize the difference between shopping for a mortgage and trying to get several new credit cards at once.

Types of credit used (diversity of credit) is 10% of your credit score. This is also called a "credit mix." Again, it shows your ability to handle different types of credit. So, if you have a student loan, a credit card, and a mortgage, you have more of a credit mix than someone who just has one credit card. There's no need to overthink this or to take out a different type of loan solely for the purpose of improving this section of your credit score. It's only 10% of it, after all.

Ultimately, your credit score is only useful if you intend to borrow money in the future. To lenders, your credit score indicates how likely you are to pay back a loan on time. If your credit score is low, lenders consider you a riskier borrower. When your score is lower, lenders will likely charge you a higher interest rate. It's their way of insulating themselves against a customer who might not repay a loan.

The worst place I see this is with car loans. If you don't have a good credit score, you can get hammered with a very high car loan interest rate. I get so angry when I hear car loan advertisements on the radio offering to get you into a car regardless of your credit score. Sometimes, these car loan interest rates can be 20% or more. In fact, if you have a subprime credit score, your car loan interest rate can be 5 to 10 times more than someone who has a prime credit score.[1] This is a huge issue because, as I mentioned in the last chapter, cars are one of the three anchors in any budget. They also depreciate in value quickly, which can create a situation in which you have negative equity in your vehicle. This is a very difficult cycle to get out of and can put you in debt that seems never ending—all for a car! This is one of the many reasons why it's important to understand how to raise your credit score.

The interest rate you get could mean the difference of thousands of dollars over the lifetime of a loan. This is especially true when it comes to borrowing money for a big-ticket item, like a home. Even a 1% higher interest rate on a mortgage could mean paying tens of thousands more dollars over the course of a 30-year mortgage loan. So, it really does pay to have a high credit score.

I should mention that you can totally be a trustworthy person who pays your bills on time but still have a low credit score. This could happen for a variety of reasons, such as if you have a very short or nonexistent credit history. For example, if you never took out a student loan or have never had a credit card, you might have a very thin credit file. Your score might show up as low in this instance simply because the credit bureaus just don't know much about you yet. But, there are all sorts of ways to build your credit and improve your score if you have a big financial goal, such as buying a house someday.

You can start by applying for credit, getting approved for credit, and paying your bills on time. You can start small with a starter credit card or a secured credit card, for example, and then build from there. The more responsible you are with your accounts, the more opportunities you'll have to build your credit profile in the future. Time helps too, since the FICO score measures the length of your credit history.

Credit scores usually go down if you are more than 30 days late on a payment, have credit utilization that's too high, or if you have too many hard inquiries on your account. A hard inquiry is when you apply for a credit card, a loan, or request a rate line increase on a credit card, and the lender checks your credit file. A soft inquiry doesn't affect your credit score. A soft inquiry might happen if an employer does a background check or if you get pre-approved for a loan. Some things, like applying for an apartment or opening a savings account could be either (it depends on the institution and you can always ask before applying).

Too many hard inquiries can negatively impact your score, but being late on a payment or having too much debt in relation to the credit you have likely has more impact on your score.

Also, it's important to keep monitoring your credit. That way, if you have a huge, unexpected drop in your credit score, you can immediately go and make sure it's not the result of identity theft.

The fastest way that I know of to raise your credit score quickly is to pay down your debt. The goal is to try to achieve less than 30% credit utilization before your creditors send their report to the credit bureaus, which happens monthly. Additionally, take care of any adverse accounts on your credit report by speaking to each account's collections department, getting current, and asking them to remove the adverse account from your report once you are. The phone number of the person you should contact should be right next to the adverse account notice on your credit report.

Once, I got denied for a credit card, and they said it was because I had an adverse account on my credit report. I was really alarmed since I always paid my bills on time, so I pulled my credit report to make sure everything was okay. Sure enough, in the adverse accounts section, there was a collections notice from the public library. I'd recently graduated from grad school, moved apartments, and in the process failed to return an audiobook to the library. (This was back in the days where we put CDs in the car on long drives. Remember those days, millennials?) I called them and they said they mailed me several notices, but they all went to my old address. They told me if I mailed the audiobook back, they would take it off my report. So, I went digging through all my moving boxes, found the audiobook, and mailed it back. In just a month or so, the collections notice was gone.

If you have a collections notice, sometimes you can negotiate with the lender and offer to pay a lump sum that's less than what you owe in order to get the collections removed. But you should always get this agreement in writing and never give them access to your checking account.

One of the biggest reasons people monitor their credit score or become interested in eliminating their debt in collections is because they want to buy a house.

Technically, you *could* buy a house with a subprime credit score (one that's below 670). But this really isn't the best idea for you (and you're the one I'm looking out for here). Many experts point to subprime mortgages as the leading cause of the 2008–2009 recession. Because of that, in the years after the recession, it was nearly impossible for subprime borrowers to get a mortgage again.

But, over the past few years, subprime mortgage loans are starting to be available again. These mortgages go by a few nicknames like "alternative mortgage programs" or "another chance mortgages" or "dignity mortgages." They often come with high interest rates.

To be honest with you, when it comes to something like owning a home, it really pays to take your time and do it right. That means working hard to learn how to manage your money, improving your credit score, saving for a down payment, and then applying for a mortgage.

Although it might be tempting to buy a house with a low credit score, especially when a lender makes a compelling case for it, try to wait. Shortcuts might get you to the destination faster, but you won't have the same level of satisfaction and security that you'll get by running the longer race.

Additionally, there's no need to try to get an 850 credit score if you want to buy a home. We're not aiming for perfection here. All you need is to work toward an excellent credit score to show banks and future lenders that you know how to handle money like a boss. Most financial experts agree that once your credit score gets to 750, you're at a place where you'll receive some of the best interest rate offers. And, you can get to a 750 credit score by paying your bills on time, having a long credit history, low credit utilization, a low number of hard inquiries, and a good credit mix.

Keep in mind, too, that when you're buying a big-ticket item like a home, lenders are looking at a lot more than just your credit score. They're also looking at your job history, your income, the amount of debt you already have, and more. A good credit score helps, but they're going to be looking at the bigger picture too.

Once you attain an excellent credit score, the best way to maintain it is to focus on payment history and utilization. Paying your credit cards on time is the most important thing you can do to keep and improve your credit score. The next best thing you can do is keep that credit utilization below 30% on each card (and ideally, at 0%.)

It's also important to continue to monitor your credit because of the increase in data breaches. Unfortunately, those happen pretty often, and if your personal information is involved in one, you could be vulnerable to identity theft.

In fact, I've been affected by those data breaches a few times, which is why I regularly monitor my credit. I actually just got an email about my information being a part of a data breach from a home design website I subscribed to. It seems like you can't even browse for living room rugs these days without your personal data being at risk.

While your first reaction might be to never trust a website again, the truth is that it's impossible to insulate yourself 100% from data breaches. What you can do, though, is be vigilant about monitoring your credit.

There are two websites I use that offer free credit monitoring: Credit Sesame and Credit Karma. These websites also allow you to see your credit score in the form of a VantageScore. Although it's not your official FICO score, the number is usually in the same ballpark and can help you keep tabs on whether your credit is improving, declining, or staying the same. What I really like is that they'll email you whenever there's a data breach involving your personal information. They'll also email you to make sure new lines of credit on your account belong to you.

So, if you get an email from one of these companies announcing that you have a new line of credit, but you didn't apply for one, you can immediately log in and dispute that change to your credit report. Sometimes these websites will offer advice on how to improve your credit score, like suggesting you apply for a new credit card or reduce your balances by a certain percentage. All of that is good information to have if you're currently monitoring and working toward improving your credit score.

If you already have credit monitoring and you're just interested in finding out your credit score, don't buy a credit score online. Surprisingly, your credit score is not listed on your credit report. They are two separate things. But, there are still many ways to find out your score for free. As I mentioned, you can get a ballpark idea of your score from Credit Sesame or Credit Karma. However, if you want your actual FICO score, which is the most well-known and used score by lenders, there are a few ways to get it.

A common way to find out your FICO score and monitor it is to get a credit card that offers this as a benefit. One of my cards emails me every month to let me know my updated FICO score is ready for me to see. Also, if you get declined for credit, you'll usually get a letter explaining why. This letter often has your credit score on it somewhere, which is a free and easy way to find out what it is.

Keep in mind there are many different versions of a FICO score. So, if you apply for a car, your auto lender will likely pull a FICO Auto Score. If you're trying to buy a house, there's something called a FICO Score 5. The FICO 8 score is still the most general and widely used score, even though a new version called FICO 10 came out in 2020.

You really don't need to know or memorize how many different types of credit scores there are, though. I only tell you that to explain why you might see your credit score as 730 in one place and then get declined by a card because they said you had a 699 credit score somewhere else. This can be confusing and frustrating when you're working hard to improve your score. But, try not to get too caught up in the *exact* number of your credit score.

Instead work hard to improve your habits, your debt-to-credit ratio, and paying your bills on time every time. Those are the elements that will ensure you have an excellent credit score all around, even if the numbers vary slightly from lender to lender. And, once you're in that

A+ excellent range, you won't have to worry as much about getting a good interest rate. That's the goal here—for moms to worry less and feel empowered about their finances.

Remember, a credit score is just a number. You can be a good person and an amazing mom and still have a bad credit score. This number doesn't define you or say anything about you. And the best news is that, if you're not happy with your credit score, you can fix it. It's not permanent. It's not a life sentence. In fact, there are only seven years of data on your credit report. If you made a mistake eight years ago, it won't be on your report anymore.

And yeah, there's a formula and there's a bunch of different factors that impact your credit score, but you can figure that out. You're smart—and as you know, you're a mom so you can do anything. Don't let the language and the rules of improving a credit score intimidate you. Frankly, I've yet to find something harder than raising my twins, so I tend to look at most things as learnable and achievable.

Lastly, remember that improving a credit score might take some time. It won't happen overnight. But, getting the courage to call creditors and negotiate is one step. Then, little daily changes to your spending is another step. Throwing an extra $50 to a credit card debt right when you get paid helps too. All these little, tiny, seemingly insignificant steps can really make a big change when you look back a year from now—or even six months from now. So, just get started, Mama, and you'll be surprised at the progress you can make if improving your credit score is one of your financial goals.

NOTE

1. Yowana Wamala, "Average Auto Loan Interest Rates: 2020 Facts & Figures," ValuePenguin, October 29, 2020, www.valuepenguin.com/auto-loans/average-auto-loan-interest-rates.

CHAPTER 6

How to Negotiate, Earn Extra Money, and Start Investing

n 2008, when my husband and I were just dating, we saved up our money from working and backpacked our way through Europe. We'd just left Florence, Italy, and he could barely get his giant backpack shut. There he was, pulling at the strings on the top of the bag trying to shove everything in so we could keep going to our next stop.

His overflowing backpack was my fault because he was helping to carry *my* things, the treasures I'd just purchased by haggling my way through the Florence markets. Those treasures, my friends, were shoes. Beautiful Italian boots kind of shoes. I bought them because I was able to negotiate with the vendors in the market, somehow making those handmade leather beauties mine on a college student's budget.

Look, I was not leaving that country without those boots, so there was no choice but to fill our packs with them as though we didn't have to drag them through several more train stations on our trip.

We laugh about it now because I was so determined and it was so long ago, when we didn't have a care in the world. Back then, I wasn't thinking about investing in the market, saving for my kids' college, or trying to remember to defrost the chicken for dinner. I was just a kid who was willing to negotiate for boots, and for the record, I still own them today.

I don't know where I learned to negotiate, but I do know it's something I've always enjoyed doing. Lots of people hate the confrontation aspect of negotiating, but I find quite a thrill in it. It's an exhilarating challenge for me, one that comes in handy as a business owner.

Apparently, I passed down my love of negotiation to my kids. Just the other day, my son lost his water bottle at school. I told him he'd have to pay me back for it, and he owed me $6. He immediately responded with, "What about if I gave you $5?" I said, "First of all, good negotiating. Second of all, no."

Even if the thought of negotiating makes you queasy, honing that skill is a necessary step to building wealth. With negotiating, you can lower your bills and get paid more. Then, the next step is learning how to invest so the money you earn and save works hard for you through the power of compound interest.

In this chapter, I'm going to teach you how to lower your bills, earn more money, and invest in your future. But first, let's talk about why it's important to do all this. Here's the deal: I want you to become wealthy.

I'm curious what your reaction was when you read that last line because for some reason, our society has made the pursuit of money into something that's negative. Watch any kids' movie and you'll notice that a lot of the bad guys are depicted as having a lot of money. Villains are often business people or bankers. So, when you spend your life absorbing media that displays the wealthy as bad, you too might associate being wealthy with being a bad person.

Even if you didn't absorb that message from the media, maybe you learned something similar from your own parents. Did you ever hear one of your parents call someone zipping around in a nice car a jerk? Did you ever think your friends who lived in huge houses were stuck up?

If so, you might have a block when it comes to becoming wealthy. After all, if your brain has had a lifetime of messaging that pursuing money is bad, then either consciously or subconsciously you might self-sabotage your ability to join the ranks of the wealthy.

So, let's talk about some reasons why it's beneficial to have more money. The three reasons that follow are my personal reasons for pursuing wealth and what I've taught thousands of other moms over the last couple of years through my business. Much as I like nice boots, making more money isn't about buying nice things. For me, it's about personal freedom, leaving a legacy, and becoming outrageously generous.

PERSONAL FREEDOM

Personal freedom is the absolute top reason why I work so hard to save money, earn more, and invest. Personal freedom, to me, means I have complete control over my life. It means I am able to earn and save enough money that I don't have to work with people who don't treat me well.

It means that I get to decide how I spend each hour of my day. It means that my life is my own. Personal freedom is the reason I became an entrepreneur. Even though I experienced a lot of highs and lows when I became self-employed, going all the way back to the grocery store incident I shared earlier, I never lost sight of why I set out on my own to begin with. I wanted to spend more time with my kids. I wanted to decide what I was going to do when I woke up and where I was going to go and when.

I was finally able to see the fruits of my labor when I went with my daughter's class on a kindergarten field trip. I sat next to her on the bus, and she spent the entire ride there *beaming*. She held my hand so tight, just squeezing it as she leaned into me. For the rest of the day, the fact that her mom came on the field trip was all she could talk about. In that moment, every single time I stayed up late to write was worth it. Every time someone was rude to me and called me cheap or obsessed with money was worth it. All the moments I said no or didn't buy something I wanted finally added up together to create the freedom to be with my child on a random weekday.

I want to be very clear; I don't pursue wealth so I can wear fancy clothes and impress strangers. I pursue it and properly manage the money I make for the freedom it brings. My daughter couldn't care less about what kind of car I drove to the school before I hopped on the bus. She just wanted me there, and the fact that I learned how to manage my money is what gave me the personal freedom to make it possible.

You don't have to be an entrepreneur to crave personal freedom or make it happen. My business is simply the method I took to create a flexible schedule and earn more. Personal freedom can be something you work toward as a family because you want to do things differently. That might mean cutting back on your spending now so you can retire early or learning how to invest to enable your family to reach financial success.

The more money you have, the more personal freedom you have. It's as simple as that. And the more personal freedom you have, the more you can invest your time in your family and helping others. I don't see anything wrong or evil about pursuing wealth. The first step is to believe you're capable and worthy of achieving it. I believe wholeheartedly that you are, but it has to be you who makes it happen.

LEAVING A LEGACY

The next reason I want to be wealthy is to leave a legacy. I don't want my kids to have to borrow money to go to college. If one of my kids wants to go to medical school like my husband, I don't want them to have six-figure loans like he does. I don't want them to spend years paying loans back when they finally get a job they've worked hard for.

Part of what I teach my kids about money will also be my legacy. Teaching them how to budget, how to plan for emergencies, how to lower their bills, and how to negotiate is also my legacy. It's about establishing a family culture where money is not taboo. It's about one day having lots of little grandkids who say, "Because of Grandma Cat, all of us went to college debt free."

My kids definitely soak up the money lessons. During the first week of first grade, their teacher asked them to put five things that represent them in a little bag so all the classmates could get to know each other. Well, in addition to a Star Wars book, a tennis ball, and a Lego, my son grabbed two pennies to put in his bag. When I asked him why he was bringing pennies, he said, "Because I love money!" That made me laugh, because clearly, I've made it so that money is not a taboo topic in my house. That said, sometimes my comfort with talking about money is a bit much for other people, especially when making a first impression. So although it made me chuckle, and I was proud, he decided to switch the pennies out for a Minecraft Lego sword and Minifigure.

Another favorite money story is the time my daughter bought herself a jean jacket when she was four years old. I rarely buy things for my kids unless it's their birthday or Christmas. We replace their clothes and shoes as they grow, but it's not often I'll buy something on a whim just for fashion's sake.

But, my daughter is super creative and loves clothes and accessories. After seeing her favorite babysitter and her ballet teacher both wear jean jackets in the same week, she decided she really wanted one too. She asked me for that jean jacket over and over again. I thought it would be a good opportunity for a money lesson, so I told her she could have it, but she had to earn the money herself.

I knew I wanted her to really work for it and not do some arbitrary task she should be doing anyway, like picking up her toys. So we agreed that, together, we would clean my car. If your car looks anything like my car, with goldfish all strewn about on the floor, then you understand why this was such a big task.

For two hours straight, we cleaned the car. Her little four-year-old self picked up trash, wiped down the insides, and used a handheld vacuum to pick up every crumb. She never complained because she was laser-focused on earning that jean jacket. When we were all finished and bought the jacket, she was radiant with pride. She took such good care of it, and she made me so proud.

Some families pass down scarcity mindsets when it comes to money. They pass down thoughts about money generation after generation that make their family afraid to invest, afraid to want more. They talk about how rich people cheat to get there and paint a picture that everyone who is wealthy is bad.

And yes, some people are dishonest when it comes to money and many people get unfair advantages. But you as the adult and as the mom get to decide what story you want to tell your kids. You get to decide how your kids view money. Your words determine what they believe is possible financially. It's your choice whether to make money a part of their life education. Personally, I hope my children and grandchildren are far wealthier and more successful than I'll ever be because of the lessons I've passed down. After all, I save, invest, and negotiate not only to make my own life better, but to make the lives better for everyone who comes after me.

EXTREME GENEROSITY

I don't feel guilty about the pursuit of money or my goal to create a better foundation for my family because extreme generosity is also in the top three reasons why I am pursuing wealth. I truly believe the more money we make, the more good we can do in the world.

Money is just an object that magnifies who you already are as a person. So, if you're naturally generous and kind, money will only enhance that. I believe so strongly in generosity that the final chapter in his book is all about the art and joy of giving. The great news is you don't have to give a lot in order to reap the benefits of being generous. You don't have to wait until there are tons of zeros after your name to start giving. Start right now with what you have, and you'll be surprised at the benefits that follow.

Now that we've established three solid reasons for pursuing wealth, we can move on to the three steps that can help you get there: reducing your bills, earning more, and investing.

REDUCING YOUR BILLS

A great way to practice negotiating is to start with your bills. Start with small things, like asking to lower your cable bill, because eventually, you'll be able to negotiate much bigger things. For example, once you get used to negotiating, you'll have no problem asking for a lower price on a car. Similarly, when buying a house, you won't feel bad asking the seller to fix things that come up in the inspection report.

One of my top tips for negotiating is to be nice. When most people think of negotiations, it might bring to mind heated discussions, which makes people nervous. But, I've had the most luck when I'm as nice as can be. Take, for example, my Internet company. Every single year they try to increase my monthly bill. And every year without fail, I call them up, sweet as can be, and ask them if they can keep my bill the same.

You have to put yourself in their shoes. In the case of my Internet company, most people who call in are probably irritated. I highly doubt that people call them and regularly ask them how their day was. So, I usually ask about them and then explain how loyal I want to be to their company. Then, I ask if that price is the absolute best they can do that day. They always try to sell me on more services, but I haven't had cable for the past decade. I only pay for high-speed Internet every month (and streaming services, of course.) Once they realize I'm quite serious and I'm not going to get cable at all, they usually help me out. Last year I even negotiated $10 less per month than I was paying before.

If I called my Internet company and yelled at them or demanded that they give me the same price as before, they're going to be much less likely to help me. The same is true if your flight gets canceled or your server completely forgot to put in your order.

All anyone wants is to be treated with kindness and respect, so if you're going to ask for something, be nice. You're much more likely to get it.

When it comes to your bills, a good rule of thumb is to call up your service companies every three to six months and ask if you're currently getting the best prices. This should only take an hour or two in the afternoon and could save you hundreds of dollars a year.

When it comes to negotiating big purchases, like a house or a car, it's helpful to collect information before you try to get a better price. You want to give yourself the absolute best chance of getting what you want, but if you lowball too much, you risk losing out. So, do your research, understand the exact value of what you're trying to buy, and try to negotiate slightly less.

Also, when it comes to big purchases, it's helpful to keep your emotions in check when negotiating. If you get too swept up in wanting to "win" you run the risk of going in the opposite direction and paying more than something is worth. There are lots of houses and cars in the world. If you can't agree on a price you're comfortable with, then it's not meant for you. Knowing when to walk away is also an important aspect of negotiating.

EARNING MORE

Once you get used to negotiating and reducing your bills, shift your focus to earning more. The combination of spending less and earning more is a surefire way to help you reach your financial goals.

The first step to earning more money is to believe that you are worthy of it.

You have to want that raise and believe it's yours with the fire of a college student who wants Italian boots. You have to be so determined that you are capable of a higher income that no one can stop you.

I remember very early on in my business trying to negotiate my freelancer rates so I could earn more. I'd get that nervous feeling in my stomach, like you get just before you go down a roller coaster, waiting to hear a client's response. Whenever they agreed to a price I wanted, it would be such a thrill.

Over the past 10 years of being in business, I've learned quite a bit about negotiating my rates after working with hundreds of people and putting together contracts with a variety of individuals and organizations.

The only reason I knew what to charge for my services is because of other people who are in the same type of business that I am. This is counterintuitive to a lot of business advice. Many people will tell you that you have to be cutthroat and aggressive in order to get ahead. However, I've learned there's so much opportunity in the world. Because of that, helping someone else by talking openly about rates doesn't take away from anyone's success.

The only way I knew what to charge as a financial writer is because I spoke to other financial writers and asked them what they charged. The only way I knew how to charge for public speaking is because I talked to other professional speakers to ask them what they charged. The same is true for any brand deal, any business contract, and even the contract terms of the book you're holding right now.

I rely on the openness of my colleagues to tell me exactly how much money they make from their work and clients. Their comfort with money and their camaraderie with me as we work to build our businesses have enabled me to grow. I'll never forget being very early on in my business and going to a conference. There, I met another financial writer in person who I'd only known online before. We shared many of the same clients, and at the conference she told me, "Hey I just asked [Client X] to increase my rate to $75 an article, and you should too."

There was nothing in it for her to give me that advice, but she did because she operates from a place of abundance. So, I went home from that conference and I asked for a raise from that client. Not only that, but I felt empowered to ask for a raise from every single one of my clients, and all of them said yes. That amounted to an increase of $1,000 a month for me in my business, which was a huge deal for me in the beginning. That same friend has sent me well into six figures of referrals and business over the past decade, and I've done the same for many other writers too.

This type of information is important, so always be willing to work with others, even if they're in the same field as you. If you work a 9-to-5 job, look at data surrounding your job title and pay in your area. When you do, you might find out someone with your job title at a similar-sized company makes $5,000 or $10,000 more per year. Or, you might find that you're on the upper end of salary for your position in your geographic area, in which case kudos to you. But either way, it's never a bad idea to ask for more. After all, you're worth it.

So, if you're working a 9-to-5 job, start by having a discussion with your boss about ways you can earn more in the future. You don't have to go into a meeting, point out that someone else at a different company makes more, and demand they match it. Instead, be your wonderful self, express your interest in using your talents to continue to help the company grow, and ask their advice on what you can do to get to the next level. Make sure you get clear guidelines on what you can do to earn more. Then, set a meeting to discuss the results three months in the future and put it on the calendar. This gives your boss time to go over their numbers and gives you time to perform at your absolute best.

If your boss isn't willing to give you advice on next steps or you've felt undervalued in your job for a long time, it might be time to search for a new one. Sometimes, switching jobs is the best way to get a big jump in salary. Don't be afraid to ask for more than you think you should get.

Actually, the metric I use is that if you feel comfortable asking for a certain salary then you're not asking for enough. Negotiating, while it can be exhilarating, is anything but comfortable.

If you're going to speak to your boss about a possible raise, it should not be a cozy, comfortable conversation. You should be the most nervous you've ever been because you're going to go in there and ask for more than what you think you deserve. Usually, this number is about right, mostly because women underestimate their value.[1] Seriously, ask for a number that makes your boss raise their eyebrows a little bit and makes them say something like, "Okay, I'll have to check and get back to you on that."

Remember, big gains and huge leaps in progress don't come from comfort zones. In other words, it always takes some level of discomfort to experience growth. Staying at the same salary for years is comfortable. Not rocking the boat or staying quiet because you're worried that you're being too demanding is the easier route. But getting to the next level, that takes a little bit of guts. It takes the roller coaster feeling. I wish I could say I've always known this innately, but it's something I learned through trial and error and the help of others.

If you're not a business owner and you don't work a 9-to-5 job but you'd like to earn a little extra money, go for the side hustle. There are so many phenomenal moms who are crushing it with their side hustles, using the extra money they make to pay off debt, start their children's college account, and invest. The great thing about a side hustle is you don't have to commit to it long term. It's something you can do for a season to reach specific financial goals. Who knows; you might enjoy it so much that it might turn into a full-time job. Even if it doesn't, it's something you can do time and time again when you need an extra financial boost.

Once you start becoming committed to the idea of earning more, there is another aspect of wealth building that's extremely important. It's not enough to just earn more money than you are currently earning. You also have to know what to do with that extra money. That's where investing comes in.

INVESTING

It's so tempting to upgrade as soon as you start to earn more. Once you get a bigger paycheck, it's easy to imagine everything you can buy with your newfound extra cash. That's why it's good to go into this journey of earning more money with a solid plan, and part of that plan should be investing.

By learning how to invest, and becoming fluent in that world, you can learn how to make your money make money. So even if your job right now is to raise humans, but you have a partner who brings home an income, you can play a valuable role in building your family wealth simply by becoming educated about investing.

Investing makes a lot of people very nervous, because they don't want to lose their hard-earned money, and that's understandable. The way I got more comfortable with investing is by learning about the history of the stock market.

When you look back at the past 100 years of the stock market, you'll notice certain trends. The stock market tends to go in cycles. It goes up and then it goes down. But, over the past century, on average, the market has returned about 10%. If you adjust for inflation to be conservative, you can call it a 7% return on average.[2]

We will all live through stock market dips and corrections in our lifetime. Sometimes the market has a terrible decade. People usually lose money when they panic and pull their money out during a downturn. But if we can look back and rely on history, we can have comfort in knowing that after a dip usually comes a rise. That's what it means to be a long-term, disciplined investor.

The easiest, most pain-free way to invest is if you have an employer-sponsored retirement plan. This is a benefit for many people working full-time jobs. I say it's pain-free because usually, you can set up your retirement contributions to automatically go out of your paycheck and into your retirement plan. You can also invest in retirement accounts outside of work-sponsored plans in a Traditional IRA or a Roth IRA. Both these investment vehicles have different tax benefits and different income limits, so it's good to take the time and do your research before choosing which is best for your personal financial situation.

If your employer matches contributions up to a certain amount, it's smart to take advantage of that because you can reach your financial independence goals that much faster. Every time you get a raise, consider increasing the percentage of your paycheck you invest (vs. increasing the amount of money you spend on other wants). I also encourage you to do your research and really understand exactly what funds you're invested in at work. Take a look at the fees you're being charged and understand how much of your hard-earned money you get to keep. Also, make sure you're actually *invested* in funds and that your money isn't just sitting in your account in cash. It usually takes an extra step to ensure you move your cash into an actual investment fund.

If you're self-employed, you can still invest in a retirement account on your own, whether that's an IRA, a SEP-IRA, or a Solo 401k.[3] If you're a stay-at-home mom, married to someone who brings in an income, and you file your taxes jointly, consider opening a spousal IRA. That enables you to have a retirement account in your own name, even if you don't have earned income yourself.

Depending on what type of health insurance you have and your employment status, you also might be able to invest in something called an HSA (health savings account) or FSA (flexible spending account). Not everyone is eligible for these accounts, but they are worth researching to see if you are because of potential tax benefits and savings on healthcare costs.

If you want to invest outside of retirement accounts, you can open a brokerage account. This is an account you can use to purchase investments like stocks, bonds, mutual funds, index funds, and more. You can do this yourself, even without the help of a financial advisor. But, if you need guidance or help with choosing funds, you can always consult one.

If you work with a financial advisor, make sure they are a fiduciary. That means they're required by law to act in your best interest rather than recommend funds or products that make them the most money. Always ask how they get paid and what percentage of your money they earn from managing your investments. You can start by searching for one with the designation of CFP® (CERTIFIED FINANCIAL PLANNER™). They have to go through rigorous testing and years of experience before becoming one.

Even if you feel intimidated by the thought of asking personal financial questions, I want to encourage you to try anyway. According to research from Mintel in partnership with Ally, women are less likely than men to seek out answers to their personal finance questions.

Additionally, their data showed women are more likely than men to believe the stock market is too risky for their investments.[4] The pursuit of knowledge is so important and the only way to learn more about money is to continuously ask questions so you can get clarification on the things you don't understand.

If you want to invest on your own, without the help of an advisor, a simple way to start is by researching different types of investments. When you do, you'll likely come across terms I mentioned earlier such as stocks, bonds, mutual funds, and index funds. You might also read about ETFs, target-date funds, and more.

I want to focus on index funds in this chapter, because it's a great place to start as a beginning investor. But first, here is a little background so it all makes sense. A stock is a piece of a company. When you buy a stock, you essentially own a little piece of Disney or Nike or whatever company you choose to invest in. When the companies do well, your stock becomes more valuable. When they don't, the value of the stock drops. A mutual fund is a collection of stocks. Instead of buying a piece of one company, you buy one mutual fund that's made up of several different companies, which spreads out the risk.

An index fund is a type of mutual fund that follows a particular index. An index is, essentially, a list of things. The index in the back of a book is a list of all the major topics in that book. The S&P 500 Index is a list of the largest 500 publicly traded companies in America.

These 500 companies are usually a good bet when it comes to long-term investing because they've already proven their success. You're not investing in an up-and-coming company that your uncle said would be a good idea. You're investing in companies that have history and a proven track record.

I mean, when it comes to hiring a babysitter, wouldn't you want one who has a lot of experience watching kids? Wouldn't you be more inclined to hire them if someone else gave them a reference? I would. I'd rather one who has had years of experience. The same is true for the companies you invest in.

Index funds are actually the type of investment Warren Buffett and many other personal finance experts recommend for their low cost and simplicity. In fact, Warren Buffett made a million-dollar bet with a hedge fund manager that investing in index funds would outperform the manager's portfolio over a 10-year period. Buffett won.[5]

Index funds are cool because they are efficient and save you brain space. If you were to buy single stocks in all 500 of the biggest companies in America, that would be a lot of work and cost a lot of money. So instead, you can buy something called an S&P 500 Index fund. It's kind of like a ready-made dinner kit, but the nice kind you can just stick in the oven, no chopping vegetables required. Instead of having to plan your meal and buy all the ingredients separately, you get the kit and have everything you need right there in a package. An index fund is similar to that. It's a package of stocks that mimics the index, something you only have to buy one of, but you get a lot of ingredients.

Theoretically, if the index it's following is doing well that day, your index fund should do well that day and vice versa. The other good thing about an index fund is that it comes already diversified since it's made up of a lot of different companies. Even if a big, well-known company has a terrible month for one reason or another, it's likely that other companies within the fund are still doing well so it balances out the risk.

There are lots of different types of index funds. You can purchase a Total Stock Market Index fund that mimics the whole market or an International Index Fund or a Real Estate Index Fund. An S&P 500 Index Fund is just one example, but it's usually a common one for beginning investors and a good place to start your investing journey.

The last perk of index funds that I'll mention is that they have extremely low fees because they are not actively managed. That means they are set on autopilot to follow an index. You are not paying for a human advisor to make changes to the fund. You can buy index funds yourself through low-cost brokerage firms. Some firms require you to have a minimum investment but that threshold to entry can be quite low, making them very accessible to new investors.

Keep in mind that there are no shortcuts or get rich schemes when it comes to investing. I'm encouraging you to research investing for the long term and to try to become educated about the process so you're not making investment decisions based on emotion.

Because I'm not a CFP® or financial advisor, I can't recommend specific funds. But, I can encourage you by saying that investing is not as intimidating as it seems. If you do anything when it comes to investing, I'd recommend reading as much as you can about the topic from as many authors as possible, preferably ones who have a knack for making investing language accessible.

It's also wise to consult an excellent accountant to see how investing affects your taxes. Be wary of taking investing advice from friends and family members who are not well versed in this topic. If an investment someone recommends sounds too good to be true, it probably is. There are many educated people who have been scammed by Ponzi schemes because they didn't ask enough questions or didn't follow their gut when they sensed something was wrong.

Choosing straightforward, conservative investments (like index funds) and buying them through well-known low-cost brokerage firms like Schwab, Fidelity, or Vanguard is usually a good way to start for a beginner. These are not the only low-cost brokerage firms, but they are examples of some of the best-known ones.

The combination of spending less, negotiating so you can earn more, and making investing part of your financial habits can turn you into a financial powerhouse. As you hone these skills and make them a part of your daily practice, pay attention to your mindset.

Notice anytime you get frustrated or any time you want to give up when your savings didn't go as planned or you didn't get what you negotiated for. Anytime you get nervous when you're trying to switch jobs or start a business, I want you to remind your own brain that wealth is possible and you are deserving of it.

If you're doing something no one else in your family has done before like start a business, make six figures, or learn how to invest at a young age, it's going to feel scary at first. But, make sure that you notice it and quickly shift to a feeling of abundance.

A lot of people subconsciously hold themselves back from earning more because they don't know what earning more will change. Will family members be jealous? Will friends treat me in the same way? How will my life be different if that happens? Sometimes people even self-sabotage and don't fulfill their potential because they're worried about what's on the other side. They talk themselves out of it because they wonder how they will handle the taxes, the responsibilities, or the pressure of becoming someone who earns more.

All these things can happen consciously or subconsciously. What's important is to take the time to self-reflect. Think back to your childhood. Think back to what you were taught about money and wealth. Try to understand how the money lessons you learned then impact your money decisions today. Decide what lessons you want to keep and decide what lessons you want to discard. Ultimately, only you can decide whether you want to be someone that leans in and increases your income.

Complacency will keep you exactly where you are. And, if you're reading this book I'm led to believe that you don't want to stay where you are. You're looking for a change. If you are looking for a push or inspiration to help you spark that change, this is it.

Most importantly, when you accept pay that is less than you deserve, you do yourself a disservice. Subconsciously, when you agree to pricing that is less than what you truly should charge, your brain will tell you things like, "See, you should have never asked for that high amount anyway. You were never going to get it."

But, when you have the courage to walk away from the opportunities that don't match your expectations, you immediately open up the world to new possibilities. When you signal to the world, "Sorry, I'm not going to accept that. I want more for my talents," the world usually aligns in your favor.

It's taken me so long to implement this rule in my business. Early on, I was so determined to grow that I would take whatever job I could, even if it wasn't for the pay I wanted. Gradually, I realized that saying no to lower-paying clients created room for higher-paying ones. It's scary at first to turn down work or to ask for more pay, but it's usually worth it.

Remember, a scarcity mindset when it comes to money means that you feel like you don't have enough. You feel like you need to hold on tight to your money. You feel like you need to take any opportunity there is to make money, even if it's something you don't want to do.

But, an abundance mindset means you believe that there is always more money to come. You always know you're going to earn more of it. You're not afraid to give it away. When you negotiate, you do so with confidence. You go into it with your full heart knowing that even if you don't get what you want, the opportunity simply was not meant for you.

Earning more, at its core, is about believing in your own self-worth. It's having the confidence to ask for what you want because you believe that you've earned it. It means you can see yourself as someone who does have a high earning potential and a boss mindset.

But remember, in order to step into a boss mindset, you have to shed any preexisting money beliefs. For example, if you're always telling yourself internally that you're bad with money, then that will continue to be your reality. If you constantly chastise yourself, saying you're an overspender, then you will keep overspending. And, if you're always telling yourself that you're broke, then that will continue to be true.

Your brain is powerful, and its job is to protect you and to keep you safe. Your brain doesn't like it when you break the status quo or try to do something new because it's hardwired for protection. So, if your brain has always learned that being wealthy is equal to being evil, then your brain will do whatever it can to keep you from turning into that. Once you change your thoughts though, you can create a new reality.

Here are some great replacement thoughts to help you as you work to spend less, earn more, and invest in your future.

Old Thoughts	New Thoughts
I really don't want to ask them to lower my bill.	What do I have to lose if I ask them to lower my bill?
The client won't come up on price.	The client is meant for someone else, not me.
I'm an impulse shopper.	I am strong enough to learn how to control my impulses.
If I negotiate, they'll think I'm pushy.	If I negotiate, they'll see how much I value my expertise.
Rich people are jerks.	The more money I make, the more good I can do in the world.
I'm scared to invest.	I'm willing to learn as much as I can about investing.
I'm scared to make a change.	Change is the only way to spark growth.

Now that we've chatted about the importance of earning more and investing, I also want to emphasize the importance of protecting your family financially as well.

NOTES

1. Katty Kay and Claire Shipman, "The Confidence Gap," *The Atlantic*, May 2014, https://www.theatlantic.com/magazine/archive/2014/05/the-confidence-gap/359815/.

2. James Royal, PhD, and Arielle O'Shea, "What Is the Average Stock Market Return?," Nerdwallet, October 26, 2020, www.nerdwallet.com/blog/investing/average-stock-market-return/.

3. "Retirement Plans for Self-Employed People," IRS, November 2020, www.irs.gov/retirement-plans/retirement-plans-for-self-employed-people.

4. "Marketing Financial Services to Women—US—October 2018," Mintel and Ally.

5. David Carrig, "Warren Buffett Wins $1M Bet against Hedge Funds and Gives It to Girls' Charity," *USA Today*, January 2, 2018, www.usatoday.com/story/money/markets/2018/01/02/warren-buffett-bet-against-hedge-funds-girls-charity/996993001/.

CHAPTER 7

Protect Your Family With Emergency Funds and Insurance

Toward the end of August back when I was 18 years old, I stood outside in the middle of the night in eerie silence. All around me, things were still. There wasn't any wind or noise. There were no snapping branches or animal sounds or pitter-patter of rain. There was just darkness. I stood out there next to my Dad, who woke me up and told me to come outside and witness a once-in-a-lifetime event—standing in the eye of a hurricane.

I grew up in south Louisiana on the north shore of New Orleans. I spent my summers as a kid digging in crawfish holes and swimming in the bayou. Hurricanes are a normal part of life there, so much so that the people of south Louisiana throw hurricane parties.

Every fall, my dad would inevitably have to board up our windows, and school and work would be canceled for a few days as the bigger storms rolled through. Then, the storms would leave, my siblings and

I would have a lot of sticks to pick up in the yard, and life would go back to normal.

But Katrina—she was different.

Hurricane Katrina came just as I headed off to college. In fact, my parents were in the middle of dropping me off in my college dorm in New Orleans when an announcement came over the loudspeakers on campus that the city was evacuating for the storm and that all parents and students should leave. So, I left all my belongings in my dorm room—mini fridge and all—and headed back home to wait out the storm as always.

I expected to return to college a week or so later, except the next morning Hurricane Katrina increased to a Category 5 storm. In a matter of days, she came through and destroyed my hometown with a vengeance. While she raged, I was tucked away in a three-story brick office building where my parents worked, which is why I was able to walk outside and stand in the eye.

A lot happened in the weeks following Hurricane Katrina, including leaving my home, which was badly damaged, switching colleges because mine closed for the semester, and watching my parents pick up the pieces of their lives.

It's all a bit of a blur, to be honest, but I remember standing in the eye very clearly. I think it's because in that moment I felt a massive sense of dissonance. Standing outside with my dad, things were still and safe and quiet. But, we both knew something big was coming. We just didn't know the impact it would have on my family's life.

Nearly 15 years after that day, as I drove to pick up my twins from kindergarten in March 2020, the same feeling washed over me. Their school, getting ready to close for spring break, told parents they weren't sure if they'd open back up or not when the break was over. We knew Covid-19 was spreading in the United States, but it wasn't quite to pandemic proportions yet.

It was a pretty day. I picked up the twins and took them home. They ran around in the backyard giggling and playing. As I watched them, in the pit of my stomach, it was almost like a string grabbed on and pulled me right back to that night in the eye of the storm. It was the same exact feeling of dissonance. There the kids were, playing and happy in the sunshine, but there was also a sense of knowing. There was something coming, and I knew the something was bad. But, in that moment, I didn't know how it would impact my life.

My college in New Orleans closed for the semester after Katrina. So, I enrolled in college in Baton Rouge instead. Similarly, 15 years later, my twins' school closed and switched to online learning due to Covid-19.

Two life-changing events—15 years apart.

We'd all be naive to think there won't be more. And, that's just in my personal life. Think of other families who've been deeply affected by war, illness, accidents, terrorism, tornadoes, fires, and floods.

These catastrophic events require large emergency funds. How prepared all of us are to weather them will determine whether our families merely survive them or actually thrive despite them.

It's not really a fun conversation, I know. And if your chest is tight from anxiety just after reading that, trust me I understand. But, because I am teaching you to develop a boss mindset, we cannot ignore this. The best-case scenario is that you build a large emergency fund and you never, ever have to use it.

The next-best-case scenario is that you have a large emergency fund and you do have to use it. And, of course, the worst-case scenario is that you and your children are caught in a situation where you have to completely upend your life because of a massive emergency, and you don't have any money to get you to a different location or to ensure that everybody is safe and taken care of.

So, how much do you need?

- If you have high-interest debt (like pesky credit card debt), start with one month of expenses in your emergency fund.

In order to figure out what you spend in one month, complete the steps outlined in the budgeting chapter, and add up all your expenses. Keep in mind, this one month of expenses can be a very bare bones budget. It does not have to include eating out or your waxing appointment. How much money do you need to stay in your home, eat, and keep the lights on? That's the goal amount for a starter emergency fund.

For most families, your starter emergency fund will have a few thousand dollars in it. For a long time, many personal finance experts popularized the idea of a $1,000 emergency fund. However, for most families, $1,000 won't get you very far. If you think about the two most common types of unexpected expenses, home repairs and car repairs, you can imagine that $1,000 would go very quickly.

Our dog recently had to spend three nights at a veterinary hospital because she was very sick, and the bill for that was about $1,500. It was a completely unexpected, out-of-the blue expense. What if I had only had a $1,000 emergency fund, which so many financial experts recommend? What would I have done about the other $500? Go into debt? Put it on a credit card? Put my dog down instead of taking care of her? And, that was just one unexpected expense. How many times have you had more than one unexpected expense pop up in a month?

Once you have your one-month emergency fund in place, shift your focus to killing that high-interest debt. Pretend the credit card debt is a roach in your house, and muster up that same enthusiasm to eliminate it! It has to go!

Once you are free from high-interest debt, then go back to your emergency fund and continue to build it until it has six-plus months of expenses in it. It sounds like a lot, I know, but your kids are worth it.

Your emergency fund could mean the difference between putting your kids in a hurricane shelter in the middle of a high school gymnasium or putting them in a hotel with a fun indoor pool to keep them busy. It seems like an unlikely scenario, but emergencies happen to families every year. And, I promise, for your kids' sake, it's worth the time it takes to double down and fill up that fund.

- If you are debt-free or you have low-interest debt (<7%), including student loans, a mortgage, or a car loan, pay your bills as you usually would but funnel all extra cash, side hustle money, and any savings you can rustle up into building up your emergency fund to six-plus months of expenses.

Why is this so vital? I would argue that it's a lack of emergency savings, rather than overspending, that causes people to get into debt in many cases.

I hear from so many moms who tell me they do the best they can with their spending. They'll tell me that they don't have a lot of designer brands and that they're cost-conscious when they're shopping for food.

However, inevitably something always comes up, which makes it very hard to get ahead. That's why emergency funds are so useful.

I know saving months of expenses might seem incredibly daunting for you, especially if you're used to a paycheck-to-paycheck cycle. And, to be fair, it is a large amount of money that I'm asking you to save, money I'm encouraging you to put somewhere else and not touch. It's money I want you to pretend isn't even there.

But, here's the good news. When you're a total boss and finally able to get that first month of emergency savings tucked away, you are going to feel *incredible*. You're going to feel like a kindergartener who got picked to be student of the day. You're going to feel responsible and most importantly, secure.

If you haven't noticed, a huge theme of this book is me trying to help alleviate your mental load. I want to help you gain back a lot of what mentally drains you. I don't want you to worry anymore. I want you to fall asleep as fast as your husband does.

So, commit to putting your first $100 in this account today. I don't care how many things you have to put on your porch and sell on Facebook Marketplace to get there. Let's do it!

Momentum is everything, so get rid of that old desk in your basement. Let go of the chair you thought would fit in the corner but really doesn't. Take that nice purse you used to use all the time but don't anymore and sell it. The second you get the money for those sales, put it right into your emergency savings account. There is nothing more important than having savings for your family. Trust me, when your house fills with eight feet of water like my childhood home did, none of the stuff inside matters. Your purses and shoes and furniture and all the art on the walls will flood, but hopefully, your kids will be safe because you saved and planned in advance.

Remember, you don't have to be in a savings frenzy forever. It can just be for a season where you decide to work overtime, do food deliveries, or purge your closets just until you get your emergency fund where you want it to be. Once you finish, you'll feel incredibly accomplished. You can pretend the fund is not there and go back to living your life, feeling confident because of what you have saved.

I keep my emergency fund in a totally separate bank account from the bank account I use for my day-to-day expenses. This reduces the likelihood that I will use it for something that is not an emergency.

Here's how I personally organize my finances. I've tried a few different ways to manage my regular checking account and my savings, and I've found this to be the most effective.

I keep all the money for my daily spending and monthly bills in one checking account. My paychecks and my husband's paychecks get deposited in this account. All our bills are set to auto-draft out of this account. There is no savings account associated with this checking account. This is simply the account where our cash flows in and out.

Then, I have another checking account and all my savings accounts at a completely different bank. With this bank, I labeled my savings accounts with different goals. There is a $1,000 mini emergency fund in one savings account and a big emergency fund in another savings account. There's a vacation savings fund, a tax savings fund, and a Christmas savings fund. I have a debit card in my wallet that's associated with this checking account. Again, I don't use it for my day-to-day expenses.

So let's say I get a flat tire, and it costs me $300 to get it fixed. When I go to pay my bill at the car shop, I can use my phone and immediately transfer $300 from my mini-emergency fund to the checking account associated with all my savings accounts. Because it's at the same bank, my transfer is instant. Then I use my debit card associated with that bank to pay my car bill.

I don't have to wait several days to move money around, and the entire transaction does not affect my main checking account and main cash flow whatsoever. It does not cause me to go over my monthly budget, and it does not cause me stress.

When it's time for Christmas, I can instantly transfer my Christmas savings fund to the checking account associated with it. Then, I can use that debit card to buy Christmas gifts. I can even do this throughout the year, like if I spot a great Christmas gift for one of my kids some other time during the year. Again, because it's all happening in a different bank from my regular cash flow, Christmas shopping does not affect my regular budget or cause me to have overages.

When it comes to emergencies, you often need to access your emergency fund quickly. So, it's not helpful to have to transfer money and wait three to four days for it to hit your regular checking account.

That's why I like having dual banks, one for my everyday expenses and one for my savings and any emergency issues.

Having this system also keeps me from accessing my savings account needlessly. Because I actually have to go in and transfer money from my savings to my checking to use it, it makes me think twice. I often ask myself, "Is this purchase worth lowering your savings account?" Or, "Is this a real emergency?"

Again, this is the system that I found works for me after trying many different ways of organizing money in the past. I have friends who have multiple checking accounts at multiple banks. But, I know that the fewer accounts I have, the better. I love streamlining my accounts, my bills, and my life. Two checking accounts works for me for this reason, and labeling my savings accounts with my goals keeps me motivated and excited.

If I were writing this book 12 months ago instead of now, I'd probably echo the advice I've been giving for years, which is to save a three- to six-month emergency fund. But, because I'm currently writing this book in the middle of the Covid-19 pandemic, it's hard to feel like that would be enough. That's why I'm pushing for a six-plus-month emergency fund. The pandemic has gone on for so long and caused such economic destruction that many Americans have used up any savings they had. According to a survey, 14% of Americans wiped out their emergency savings because of the pandemic and 11% borrowed money to cover everyday expenses.[1]

For many families, a large-scale emergency hasn't really been at the forefront of their minds, so this has all been quite a shock. After all, prior to this pandemic, the American economy was booming. Job growth was good. The stock market blew past all expectations. But now, things are uncertain, and they can change in a matter of weeks. That's why it's always good to have money saved on the side. You need it for your sanity, but you also need it to protect your kids. Saving for an emergency won't happen overnight. It might not even happen in a month or two. However, don't let that stop you from starting. And once you start, don't quit until it's done.

Now that we've covered emergency funds at length, it's time to look at insurance. I feel like this is one of the least fun things about becoming an adult. But, if you have kids and people who rely on you, buying term life insurance is an incredibly important step.

There are a lot of different insurance products out there so make sure you're reading the fine print. I recommend term life insurance, not whole life insurance or any other type of life insurance that has a different name. Whole life insurance salesmen will regale you with tales of how buying whole life insurance is an investment and how your money will grow. But, they rarely tell you how much money they make if they sell you the product or what fees they'll charge you. Insurance should be insurance, not an investment opportunity.

Whole life insurance salesmen also do a great job of trying to get you to buy life insurance for your kids. They tell you that you can use it as a savings account and then use the money for college. Again, insurance should be insurance. It's not a good investment account. If you want to save money for your kids' college, save it in a college savings fund like a 529 plan or an Education Savings Account (ESA). If you insist on having life insurance for your child, you can ask your term life insurance provider if you can buy a rider for your child.

When it comes to term life insurance, purchase a policy that is somewhere between 10 and 12 times your annual income. So if your income is $50,000 a year it's wise to get a policy that's worth anywhere from $500,000 to $600,000.

This is also important to get if you are a stay-at-home mom. I meet a lot of stay-at-home moms who never even considered buying a term life insurance policy for themselves. But, think about everything that you do for your family and how valuable your work is. If something happened to you unexpectedly, it would cost a considerable amount of money to hire someone to do everything that you do for your family. Childcare alone would be incredibly expensive.

So, whether you're a stay-at-home mom, a single mom, a working mom, or some combination of all of these, make sure that you get quoted for a term life insurance policy. If you have a policy through work, it might not be large enough to take care of your family if something should happen to you. So, please consider getting a policy that's adequate.

If you are unable to get a term life insurance policy due to medical conditions you may have, there might be alternative options available to you that you can find through independent research. At a minimum, you can set aside the money you would have spent on policy premiums in an investment account specifically for that purpose.

This is also a good time to set up a will if you don't have one already. If you're worried about the expense and you don't have a complicated estate, there are many low-cost options and apps that can help you create a basic will. If you have a more complicated estate, hire an estate-planning attorney to help you.

I'm also a huge advocate for creating an emergency binder, something that you can keep on your computer digitally and in hard copy form in your house. You're the mama, so if something happens to you, your family is going to need a lot of support and help picking up the pieces. An emergency binder can be a good first step to getting your life organized and doing some bosslike "adulting." Not only can you include basic information about your household and you, but you can include information about your kids too if someone needs to step in and take over.

Things to Include in an Emergency Binder

Bank account information and passwords
Investment account information (this is a good time to check your beneficiaries)
Life insurance information
Disability insurance information
Health insurance details
Computer and phone passwords/codes
Medical power of attorney form
Health insurance information
List of children's medical providers, vaccination records, etc.
Car insurance information
Copies of car titles or account information for car loans
Account information for student loans
Email and social media passwords

Accountant's contact information
List of babysitters and their contact information
List of credit cards with login information
Description of how you envision a memorial service for you
Will and trust information, attorney contact information
Location of other important documents or safety deposit boxes
Any other personal information you'd like your family and your children to know

Because your emergency binder will have sensitive information in it, like your bank passwords and account information, keep it in a safe place and only let one or two trusted people know where it is. Update it every few months so that it has the most accurate information in it.

Between your emergency binder, securing a term life insurance policy, and building your emergency savings, you will acquire a great sense of peace and be able to take care of your family in a worst-case scenario.

NOTE

1. Erin Pinkus, "CNBC|SurveyMonkey Poll: 'Invest in You' August 2020," www.surveymonkey.com/curiosity/cnbc-invest-in-you-august-2020/.

CHAPTER **8**

The Childcare
versus Career
Dilemma

All I could hear were the sounds of both of my two-year-olds sobbing and banging on the window. Their cries had something to do with the fact that I had to step outside on my front porch to give a radio interview. This wasn't just any radio interview. It was my first spokesperson job for a company that hired me to complete 10 different radio interviews on their behalf over a period of two days. The interviews were national segments with tens of thousands of listeners and wouldn't you know, my babysitter couldn't be bothered to wake up that morning to watch the twins so I could do it.

I'd just moved to Michigan, and my entire house was full of boxes. It wasn't the greatest time for me to accept a spokesperson job, but it was such a big opportunity, I couldn't turn it down. With my husband working very long hours at the hospital as a new intern, I had to scramble to find a babysitter in a state where I didn't know a soul.

The babysitter I hired was a teenager who was off from school for the summer. She seemed very excited to help and had experience.

I even talked to her parents. But the morning of the radio interviews came and there was no sign of her. She didn't answer her phone or texts, and I found myself in my house with two two-year-olds not exactly sure how I was going to make it all happen. After all, this was before much of the world had to learn how to work at home with kids in the house, so I wasn't sure how my client would react if my kids interrupted the radio programming they paid me to do. (I think people are more understanding now in a Covid-19 world.)

Either way, I ended up giving the interviews on my front porch. If you've had a two-year-old, you'll know it's very different from having a six-year-old or a 10-year-old. They're not very self-sufficient. And, although I knew I could get at least two of the interviews done during their nap, there were still several others I had to figure out how to give—like a professional—without two kids crying in the background.

These radio interviews were live and scheduled segments, so there was no option to move them. I came up with the idea of doing the segments outside because I thought I could put on a show for the kids, quietly step onto the porch to do the interview, and watch them through the three huge windows we have in front of our house.

Well, the twins didn't like that idea very much. The show held their attention for about three minutes, and then right about the time I went live on the air, they realized that I was, in fact, not in the room with them. There was no show that could capture their attention once they realized that their mom was somehow gone. When they spotted me through the window as I smiled and waved at them, they were not smiling—not at all. They both stood at the window sobbing and banging on it. To them, I was in mommy jail, stuck outside. They didn't know that mommy had to put herself outside so I could be live on the radio, speaking on behalf of a billion-dollar insurance company.

I'm not going to lie; I had a lot of self-doubt that day. I didn't feel like a professional business owner. I didn't feel like a great mom. I felt like I was simply posing as a real adult but in reality shouldn't be allowed to be in charge of anything (or anyone.) But, I made it work as best as I could in those 15-minute interview chunks, and the kids and I survived that day, even though all of us had tears at some point.

What mattered is that I did my job well and the kids were safe because I could see them through the window the whole time I worked.

Remarkably, no one who interviewed me or the tens of thousands of listeners that day had any idea that my babysitter failed to show up that day.

What can I say? Quality childcare at affordable prices is very hard to find. This is a burden for so many families and something that can prevent you from pursuing your dreams, whatever they may be. Sometimes, people have family members who can help them with childcare tasks. For us, because we live many, many states away from our family members, we haven't had that available to us on a regular basis.

When I was pregnant with my twins, I had it all mapped out. My plan was to be a stay-at-home mom who worked on my business whenever my kids napped and after they went to bed. I thought I could do everything on my own, without outside help. I believed I'd be saving my family money on childcare and building my career at the same time all while keeping my house clean and my two infants happy. Not only that, but I'd be able to witness every one of my kids' milestones. Perfect, right?

Well, it was a dream from someone who had no concept of how challenging it was to raise children. As you'll find out in the next chapter, things didn't quite work out as planned. Eventually, I realized I couldn't be everything to everyone, at least not successfully.

So, I hired a mother's helper when my twins were babies for $10/hour. She was a sweet high school junior who came over after school two days a week to help me feed the babies, clean bottles, and help in any other way she could. That was the childcare I could afford at the time, and it was just enough to take the edge off and have a little help with the twins. Her help allowed me to breathe, to see the light again. As an unexpected bonus, her family adopted us, inviting us over for holiday dinners and Fourth-of-July parades. So, not only did we get our very first bit of childcare help through her, but we gained her family as friends during the process too.

At that point, I did something I call "reinvest in the babysitter." Every time I was able to earn money or complete a writing job while I had childcare, I took some of that money and added childcare hours. So, when my mother's helper first started, I could only afford to have her for what equated to $160 a month. But, as I slowly grew my business I'd earn money and then add to her hours, which enabled me to pitch more and earn more again. I continued this until I was able to hire someone to come during the day, not just after school. Eventually, I was able to have someone help with my kids 25 hours a week. I continued with that schedule until my kids started school full-time.

As such, I have a unique perspective when it comes to both stay-at-home moms and working moms as I've been straddling those two worlds since my kids were born. Even though I had bad luck with the new babysitter I chose the morning of those radio interviews, we did have great luck with many others who enriched our family and loved our kids.

I know that finding quality childcare and paying for childcare is a core issue for parents. And, it's no secret that there needs to be so much improvement on a national scale in the United States when it comes to family leave and maternity leave. But, until that happens, we all have to find childcare solutions that work for our individual families and fit into our personal budgets.

For some people, that means heading into work full-time and finding a great daycare or nanny to take care of your kids. For others it means finding a part-time babysitter and seeking a flexible job, which is the route I took. Additionally, many moms will decide to leave work and stay home with their kids.

I often hear moms say they decided to stay home with their kids because after paying for childcare, they wouldn't have had much left over from their paychecks. But, that's where things get tricky, at least in a financial sense.

If you want to be a stay-at-home mom because it's something you believe in and want to do, I think that's amazing. I'm a huge advocate for stay-at-home moms. I designed my entire career around being able to work from home so I could see my kids more. So, I completely relate to the desire of wanting to see your kids during the day, pick them up from school when they get older, volunteer in their classrooms, and more. So I very much understand the draw of this choice.

But, if your main reason for wanting to stay home is because your take-home pay is more or less equivalent to your childcare bills, you're leaving out some important math.

If your employer offers you benefits, there's quite a big difference between your gross pay and net pay. Your gross pay is the money you make before your benefits in any retirement contributions are taken out. If you take advantage of an employer-sponsored retirement plan, that will be taken out of your paycheck before you get it. The same is true of social security, health care, and anything else you've elected to have automatically taken out of your check. Only after all of that is taken out do you get your net income. That's the amount of money deposited in your bank account. Whenever I talk to moms about the financial decision of staying home, they are typically referring to their net income when comparing it to the cost of childcare.

The problem with that comparison is that it's not reflective of your total compensation package. In order to truly compare the cost of childcare with what you earn at your job, you need to look at your gross income. It's also important to talk about whether you will still be able to invest if you decide to stay home. Can your spouse open up a spousal IRA for you so you still have retirement contributions in your name? How much will it cost if you have to get a different health insurance plan, dental plan, or vision plan?

Additionally, what is your earning potential? How often does your employer give raises? What does someone make in your position who has 5 to 10 more years of experience? What will happen to your earning power if you step out for 1 year, 5 years, or 18 years?

As you can see, comparing your net income to the cost of childcare is too simplistic. If you're looking at the numbers and taking emotion out of it, you have to gather more information. Will you be losing out on investing time? Will taking yourself out of the workforce set you back in terms of raises? Will you be able to retire when you want if you step out of the workforce right now? Will you be able to raise your kids with the lifestyle you want them to have if they have just one working parent? Do you have a plan of what you'll do in the event of a divorce, death of a spouse, or your own health emergency?

Some of these questions are not easy ones, and I know they force you to think of some worst-case scenarios, things you can't even fathom right now. But, things do happen, and I'm an advocate for all moms, so

I want to make sure that if you do become a stay-at-home mom that you always have financial awareness and financial protection in case of an emergency.

It might seem like I am advocating for moms to work at a job and keep working, but that couldn't be further from the truth. What I'm advocating for is that you make decisions with full knowledge of the financial impact of your choices. I'm pushing you to run the numbers and to think about your finances not only in the present but also in the future. I want you to still have investments in your own name even if you decide to stay at home. My hope is to encourage you not to completely step out of the financial conversation even if your day is filled with toddlers wreaking havoc on your house. Remember, one of the greatest gifts you can give your kids is to be financially independent and not a financial burden *to them* when you are older. You have to know what's going on. You have to ask the hard questions.

So, what that means is that if you choose to be a stay-at-home mom, which is a valid choice, you understand the financial impact that will have on your family. It also means you are committed to taking the lead and speaking with your partner about how you will handle money together once you stop working. Before you make the switch, you need to discuss what will change about your monthly budget. It's important to establish whether each of you will continue to have some type of allowance where you are able to buy things for yourself without question or critique. Sometimes, in relationships where only one spouse is working, there becomes a power shift where the earner feels like because they are working, they get to make every money choice. I want you to still feel like a financial boss, even if you're covered in spit-up.

As a stay-at-home mom who is learning to manage money like a boss, it's important to advocate for yourself, to show that even though you may not be earning a paycheck, the support and services you provide for the family are incalculable. You still get a say in your partnership, in your spending, and in your budget. I encourage you to spend time educating yourself about managing money and investing. I want you to take a seat at the table and to help lead your family to a brighter future.

If you make the choice to be a stay-at-home mom to save money on childcare, I don't want you to lose your autonomy. It takes a lot of communication between partners to elegantly navigate a relationship where one person stays home to take care of children and the other works. There's a lot of pressure on the working parent to provide as well because the financial needs of their entire family rest on their shoulders and their ability to do their job well.

Plus, it's very easy to slip into resentment and exhaustion when you're home with little kids all day and you need a break, but your partner has been at work all day and also needs some downtime. If you add financial worries and stress to resentment and exhaustion, it can be a recipe for disaster in your personal life. So, you have to have some built-in mental breaks for both partners and the ability for some freedom and autonomy when it comes to spending as well. There is a way to harmoniously stay at home with your kids, but it will take some financial backing and open communication to make it work.

For the record, I see nothing wrong with hiring a babysitter every now and then if you're a stay-at-home mom. Put it into your budget not for anyone else but for you. If you can't fit it in, trade childcare with another stay-at-home mom so you each get a little break. A lot of stay-at-home moms feel like they should do everything, but it's incredibly difficult to be home with little kids all day. This adds to the mental load, to the exhaustion. So, when you have a budget meeting, advocate for yourself. See if you can fit two to three hours of babysitting a week into your budget so you can take a drive, go grocery shopping alone, or spend time getting coffee with a friend without interruption.

Just because you don't have an actual paycheck hitting your bank account doesn't mean that you can't have a break from time to time. People who work 9-to-5 jobs get vacation time and sick time. Stay-at-home moms are on the job 24 hours a day, 7 days a week. So don't feel badly about asking for some perks every now and then. Your mental health is an absolute priority when it comes to your family's overall happiness. You know it, and I know it, and you should never feel guilty about designing your life to ensure you have personal space from time to time.

Unless you have an exceedingly high household income, slimming down to a one-income family usually takes a lot of compromise, planning, budgeting, and sacrifice. It's absolutely worth it if staying home with your kids is something you deeply want and care about. But, it's not as simple as looking at your paycheck and comparing it to the cost of daycare. Instead, I want to empower you to become a total financial boss and to run every single number possible before you make this major decision.

Similarly, if you are a working mom, there's going to come a point where you will need to outsource in order to make things work. Working moms still get woken up in the night by little voices even after they've put in a full day at the office. Motherhood is an all-encompassing role, and you will often need back up. If you have a partner, hopefully they help keep things running smoothly. But, if you're both working long hours, you'll likely still need to outsource something. If you're a single mom, it's almost certain you'll need to outsource various tasks or rely heavily on your family and community in order to parent and work successfully.

The biggest outsourcing cost for working parents comes in the form of childcare when your kids are under age five and not in school yet. The Economic Policy Institute shares childcare cost data from every state. In Michigan, where I live now, the average annual cost of infant care is just under $11,000 at the time of writing. In New Jersey, where I lived before, it's nearly $13,000. In Louisiana, where I grew up, it's just over $7,700 annually. In California, it's just under a whopping $17,000 per year.[1]

Plus, childcare is a budget category where quality matters the most (and quality matters deeply to millennials). So, I know it's a huge challenge to find childcare providers you are comfortable with. We usually interview several candidates, and I love seeing how they interact with our kids. I won't hire someone who doesn't acknowledge my kids. It's the people who ask the kids questions and seem to want to play with them during an interview that tend to do the best work for us. When it comes to childcare facilities, preschools, and schools, the happiness of the people who work there is also an important indicator. If caretakers seem tired, cranky, or you can overhear them complaining about the kids or their boss, it might not be a good environment.

Ultimately, I know it's hard to find a place you feel safe leaving your children, especially one that is affordable. If you just moved somewhere or feel like there are limited options, don't be afraid to reach out to local mom groups on Facebook, neighbors, or other moms at your children's activities. Sometimes, you can find the best childcare simply by word of mouth. They might be able to tell you about an in-home daycare in the neighborhood or a nanny who is ready to switch families. Remember, it's okay to ask for help, especially in a budget category as important as this one.

Of course, the need for childcare doesn't end when your kids start school. Even once your children are school age, you'll likely still need to spend money on after-school care, babysitters, or after-school activities to cover the hours between when they're off from school and you're off from work. Plus, as kids get older, they tend to take on more extracurricular activities, which can get expensive.

Travel sports teams, extensive dance practices, multiple instruments, drama club, and more all take coordination not only of your time but of your wallet too. Right now, my kids are little and we've limited them to just one after-school activity each, but I know it's only a matter of time before their interests grow and they want to add new things.

According to a 2019 survey, 46% of parents spend more than $1,000 every year on their children's extracurricular activities and 62% of them have been in debt due to their kids' activities.[2] So, when you are weighing the cost benefits of whether to stay at home, consider your lifestyle needs now and in the future. Babies don't join competitive gymnastics teams, but elementary-age school kids do. So, when running the numbers and deciding on your goals, consider the cost of any future lifestyle shifts that might need to incorporate your children's interests, preferably without going into debt to make it a reality.

Another popular area of the budget to consider outsourcing is food, and this goes for every mom out there. Depending on the age of your kids, each member of the family can select a night that they're responsible for dinner. You can also make a meal plan, prep food for the week, or even order dinner a few times a week if you're able to fit that into your budget. One thing my husband contributes is going to the grocery store because it's a task I really don't like doing. It saves me time and stress. He also tries to think about dinners, which again, saves me the mental space.

I don't mind prepping simple dinners like tacos or spaghetti, but creating the ideas in my mind is always difficult for me. Maybe you're different and love looking up recipes and planning what you're going to buy at the store. If so, go with that. Play to your strengths, and then try to outsource the rest either to your kids, your other half, or some wonderful local restaurant.

Regardless of what you outsource, the important lesson of this chapter is to ask for help when you need it. Keep referring to your budget if you want to add in something to outsource and see if it makes sense for your cash flow.

A good rule of thumb is to outsource what you like doing the least. So, if you were to think of all the household and child responsibilities you're responsible for, list them in order of what you like to do best to least. Some moms love party planning. Some love organizing. Some love helping their kids with their homework. I happen to have one friend who really enjoys vacuuming. Other moms enjoy hiring tutors, housekeepers, and the occasional party planner. I always say I love to read to my kids. It's one of my favorite things to do as a mom. But, I don't want to make a volcano or create slime. Just know what you like to do, what you'll tolerate, and what you might really enjoy outsourcing. Give yourself that gift, whether you work outside the home or not.

We might not be able to outsource every single task in our lives. That's just a budgeting reality. However, if you can outsource just one task you don't like, you'll create more time and space for more of the things you love. That creates more harmony in your mind, which can lead to more patience and less chaotic evenings. Who wouldn't want that?

So, if you're in a position where you're pondering a change in terms of your career or your childcare situation, consider all factors. Working moms might need to spend more money on outsourcing. Moms who stay home will likely experience a drop in income or lost investing time. Although it's important to follow your heart and do what you believe is best for your children, remember that providing them a financially stable home is of prime importance. That might mean cutting back and paying closer attention to your budget if you decide to stay home. Or, it might mean leaning into work more to earn more income while utilizing childcare.

The choice will look different for everyone and every family, and I respect every mother for the choices they make. My role is not to recommend a specific path but to empower you to run all numbers before making big choices. That way, you can confidently lead your family to the life and lifestyle you believe is best for them.

NOTES

1. "The Cost of Child Care in Michigan," Economic Policy Institute, October 2020, www.epi.org/child-care-costs-in-the-united-states/#/MI.
2. Matt Schulz, "8 In 10 Parents Think Kids' Extracurricular Activities May One Day Lead To Income," CompareCards, www.comparecards.com/blog/8-in-10-parents-think-kids-extracurricular-activities-may-lead-to-income/.

CHAPTER **9**

Finances in Your Relationships

The smell of coffee was intimately familiar as I settled into a seat in the corner of my local coffee shop. I took out my computer and held my fingers over the keys, a stance I'd been in hundreds of times over many years. But, I didn't quite feel like myself that day. In fact, I hadn't felt like myself in months, ever since my twins were born. After the babies spent time in the NICU, we moved across the country away from family. I'd been in pure survival mode trying to care for them, keep my business running, and support my husband as he started his clinical rotations at the hospital.

I was trying to get back to who I was, though, and reaching for what was familiar. The laptop. The coffee. The keyboard I knew so well with the "a" slightly rubbed off from hitting it a couple million times while writing.

I was proud of myself for getting out of the house that day. Before then, leaving my twins felt odd—reckless even. They were so tiny, and I, as their mom, felt like I should be the one to be there for them always. But, I knew in order to get back to being me, I had to lean into the truest part of me, which was writing. I had to get back somehow to who I was before, so that my kids could get to know the real me, the one with ideas and words and passions.

Plus, I left them in the caring hands of my husband, who was a third-year medical school student at the time. I knew he was the best person to watch them, while I stepped away for just an hour or two to get some work done.

But, as my fingers hovered over the keyboard, I found I couldn't instruct them to actually come down and press the keys, because in that moment, the thoughts came.

The thoughts were unwanted and deeply troubling with crisp details about awful, terrible things happening to the kids. *"It's not really happening. They are with their dad. They are safe. Get to work,"* I told myself. And yet, as hard as I tried, I just couldn't push them away.

I picked up the phone and called my husband. "Are the twins okay?" I asked nervously. "Yeah, they're great," he said, "You've only been gone five minutes. They're still bouncing away in their bouncers just like they were when you left. Why?"

I didn't want to tell him why, but for some reason, this time I felt compelled to. "It's just," I said, "I had this overpowering thought that they were ... hurt—in pain. It was so real it took my breath away. I can't write like this."

There was a long pause on the line, and he said, "Catherine, how often do you have thoughts like that?" And I admitted, "All the time ... Actually, I've had them ever since they were born."

Another long pause.

And then, with the calmness and the kindness my husband is known for, he said, "Babe, I think you might need some help. I'm going to find someone who can help you."

And so began my journey to recognizing I'd been quietly suffering from postpartum depression (PPD) and postpartum obsessive compulsive disorder (OCD). The unwanted thoughts that came all on their own were torturing me, and I didn't let anyone know for months.

The primary reason I'm such an advocate for mental health in motherhood is because I let mine slip without telling a soul. It's why I'm pro-outsourcing, pro-budgeting, and pro-wellbeing. I know it's deeply important for moms to take care of themselves, to recognize when their mental load is too much. I can see it so clearly now in retrospect, but when I was deep in it, I didn't realize how bad off I was.

To this day, I thank my husband for not judging me and for taking care of me that day, for finding me a kind doctor who listened to me and helped me get back on a path to good health.

Why do so many of us quietly suffer? Why do we pretend we are okay when we aren't? By the time I got help for my PPD, I couldn't even think of a friend to call. Caught up in the needs and care of my two babies, I'd neglected to keep up with any of my friends. And, the longer I went without talking to people, the more I felt anger and shame. "Why isn't anyone calling me and asking about me? Don't they know I'm struggling?" I'd wonder. Then, I'd think, "It's a good thing no one called me today. Otherwise they'll hear me cry, then gossip about how I'm an unfit mother."

Now, I recognize that was just the depression talking, playing tricks on my brain, trying to keep me isolated and alone. Depression makes you think no one cares about you. It makes you feel like if you did share your feelings, you'd be bothering someone or wasting their time. It also makes you think no one would want to be friends with you. After all, don't people want to be friends with outgoing, positive, happy people? Why would they want to talk to someone who is such a downer?

Not only that, but why would someone call and ask me if I'm okay when all of my social media profiles showed otherwise? All I did was post adorable pictures of my twins on Facebook. I didn't look like someone who was in need of any help. Although I did write a blog post about how I needed to find more balance and I got some very supportive comments, I didn't quite share the full story. I didn't share the depth of what was plaguing me for fear of what they'd say.

When I think about it, I see so many parallels between my experience with PPD and money. Our society has made it taboo to talk about both money *and* mental health. So, when we're having a problem in one of those areas, we're conditioned to say nothing. Not only that, but we silently feel so much shame, even though mental health struggles and money struggles are both incredibly prevalent. Still, we want our friends and family to see us as successful. We want to project the image that everything is okay. We want to make sure everyone knows we're good mothers, that our children are safe with us.

But, the truth is, if we can't be vulnerable and share our struggles with others, we might never get the support necessary to improve. Having solid relationships you can count on is not simply a *want* when it comes to your financial and emotional success. It's a need.

When it comes to your money, you have to have the courage to let people know not only when you're struggling, but when you're working on a big financial goal.

Whether you realize it or not, your financial success relies on the strength of your personal relationships. It also relies on you having the confidence to set boundaries and stand your ground when anyone tries to convince you to do something you're not comfortable with financially.

For example, let's say you want to become debt-free and you start to tell your friends and family about your big, audacious goal. In a best-case scenario, your friends and family are extremely supportive of you. They understand you might not be able to go out to eat or participate in big family trips. They share budget-friendly recipes with you and ask you if you need anything to help you achieve your goals.

In this best-case scenario, your friends and family don't make you feel ashamed of the financial hole that you're in. Maybe some of them will even be inspired and join you on the journey to financial freedom. It's quite possible you'll influence many of them to have more potluck dinners instead of fancy meals out. Perhaps with your leadership and guidance, they'll also start shopping for secondhand clothes for their kids and canceling subscriptions.

But, unfortunately, not every scenario is a best-case scenario. When you are vulnerable and share your financial situation and financial goals with those closest to you, you have to also be prepared for some resistance. Most people think that debt is a fact of life, something that will always be there no matter what. They might not like your new goal because it highlights their own insecurities when it comes to their personal finances. You might have family members give you massive guilt trips for not going on family trips or not giving elaborate enough wedding gifts. They might call you cheap or stingy, which will make you second-guess why in the world you decided to be vulnerable to begin with and tell them about your financial plans.

But here's the thing. Vulnerability puts *you* in control. Vulnerability is something that you, as a mom with a boss mindset, can utilize to get back in the driver's seat and take charge of your next steps. It might not feel that way because sharing our most intimate struggles or biggest money goals can be anxiety inducing, but it's true. When you don't tell people you're struggling, it causes you to burrow further inward. It makes you feel like you want to hide, and you let the shame take over. Similarly, when you keep those big audacious financial goals to yourself, like how you really want to pay off your house in your thirties, it's easy to talk yourself out of it or convince yourself you're not worthy or capable of something so big.

Keeping these goals and dreams to yourself makes you feel like something is wrong with *you* for wanting them. When you share them out loud, two things can happen. You can find your people—those who will support you, champion you, or help you reach your goals. Or, you'll find the detractors, the haters, the ones who don't believe it's possible. That's useful too because you'll know exactly who you can confide in and who you can trust. Plus, it shifts that feeling that something is wrong with *you* onto them. No one is saying your friends and family have to jump on your money-saving bandwagon. But, if they can't be kind and supportive of your journey, that says something about their hearts, not yours.

Who you spend your time with, who influences you, who you entrust with your money dreams can quite literally make or break your financial success. Wouldn't you rather have a cheerleader, someone who supports you when you're finally ready to share how financially successful you want to be? Well, you won't know who that person will be until you commit to vulnerability, until you finally step out and stop facing your struggles alone.

Let me give you a few scenarios that you might relate to.

Sarah's brother is having a destination wedding in Jamaica, and he wants his entire family there. He and his future bride booked their wedding in Jamaica because having his ceremony and reception there at an all-inclusive resort is far less expensive than having a big bash in their home city of Chicago. Sarah's brother expects his family to buy their own plane tickets and pay for their own accommodations. The only problem is Sarah is saddled with credit card debt. She has no way of paying to attend the wedding, but all of her family thinks she is financially successful. Sarah is ashamed to let them know she can't afford the trip. She doesn't even think she has enough space on her credit card to book one plane ticket for just her, let alone for her partner and two kids, who her brother wants to be in the wedding.

This is a tricky situation for Sarah. After all, it's her brother's wedding! But she really can't afford to go. She's worried about being vulnerable and telling her family because she doesn't want them to be disappointed in her. But the thing is, if she lets them know she can't fit it into her budget, they just might surprise her. Her dad might have tons of airline miles that he hasn't used yet that he'd be happy to gift her. Or, her cousin, who would love to have Sarah's handy partner help finish her basement, might exchange paying for plane tickets for a few weekends of help with home improvements. Perhaps a family member will offer to help Sarah list and sell things in her house so she can earn enough money to get to the wedding. Maybe Sarah will earn enough money selling items to go to the wedding by herself, without her partner and kids. That way, at least she doesn't disappoint her brother but she also doesn't max out her credit card and risk her financial future. (Plus, in that last scenario she gets a little me-time, which makes it my favorite choice.)

Maybe these things would happen and maybe they wouldn't if it was your family or your friends. But, I do know that disappointing other people is a better option than disappointing yourself and putting your future at risk. It's true; other people might not understand your choices and that's okay.

For example, if Sarah decided to go to the wedding by herself because that's all she could afford, she might have disappointed her mom who wanted to see her grandbabies dressed up as flower girls.

But Sarah, who decided she was going to take charge and manage her finances like a boss, decided getting financially savvy so she could better support her kids one day was more important than having her children in a few family wedding pictures. (Plus, who knows if the kids would have made it through the evening ceremony without crying anyway.)

Money is rarely black and white. Sometimes you have to make hard choices and disappoint people in order to keep your financial house intact. But, the good news is that when it comes to hard decisions like attending family events, there is typically some room for compromise. And, everyone is different. Maybe your brother is your best friend in the entire world, and you'd be willing to work for six months at a retail store on the weekends just so you can pay to go to his wedding. Or, maybe he's the type of person who will completely understand if you can't fly four people to Jamaica even if you have adequate notice. After all, that is a big ask. Maybe he'll be understanding and gracious when you tell him that what you *can* afford is taking him and his new wife to a beautiful, elegant $100 brunch—your treat—when they get back from their honeymoon. Perhaps you'll sit together sipping mimosas and hear all about how the cake almost toppled over and how they had to run through the airport to catch their flight after oversleeping.

As women, we are conditioned by society to please, to do what we're told, and to make things easy on others. We're so worried about being a bother, about being guilt-tripped by family members, that we inconvenience ourselves to make others' lives easier. Sometimes that includes taking on a financial burden we don't want, just to avoid confrontation or hurting someone's feelings. This has to stop.

The mental load of trying to keep everyone else happy drains you of your energy and makes you untrue to yourself. When you decide to step into a boss-mom mindset instead, it enables you to speak up and set boundaries, while still leaving room for kindness. It helps you to say, "No one wants to go to Jamaica more than I do. I want to go on vacation like, yesterday. But the thing is, I won't be able to fit it into my budget and still pay for x, y, and z. Yes, I know this is disappointing to everyone, but this is the decision I made. I can't wait to see the pictures and hear all about it."

Another follower asked me about going out to eat with her girl-friends. She said, "Every time I go out to eat with my friends, they choose really expensive restaurants and order several drinks each. I can barely afford to go out, but I'm worried if I don't go, they'll stop inviting me. How can I keep my friends but also not come across as the cheap one?"

I can relate to not wanting to be seen as the cheap one. But, to me, there is a big difference between being cheap and being frugal. Cheap means you're stingy; it has a negative connotation. It means you hate parting with your money and you're only concerned with cost, not quality. Frugal means you spend based on your values. This woman doesn't see the value in going out to eat at expensive restaurants and ordering several drinks with her friends. She clearly likes her friends because she's worried about being excluded. So, my advice is to offer an alternative. Again, there's always room for compromise.

I would suggest that she propose a night in where she and her friends try some fun cocktail recipes at home. They can order take out or cook something together. The quality time will still be there as well as the food and the drinks. However, it's guaranteed to be less expensive because you won't have the restaurant markup. Chances are, she might not be the only friend who feels this way. There are likely one or two other women who are looking at their bank accounts and wishing they had more money in them, but they don't want to be the one to suggest something new. By adopting a boss mindset and being the one to lead this new form of spending time together, she can save money and still keep her friends.

However, if her friends give her a hard time about this suggestion or if they accuse her of being cheap, then they weren't that great of friends to begin with. I'd encourage anyone who is worried about a situation like this to adopt an abundance mindset when it comes to your relationships. There are over seven billion people in the world. You don't have to spend time with people who make you feel less, who call you names, or who give you a hard time for trying to make your life better. You're an adult and you're a mom. Sometimes you'll have to make hard choices about who you spend your time with, and that's okay. The more confident you get and the more sure you are of your goals, the easier it will be to stand your ground. And, I think once you do, you'll be surprised at the number of people who feel the same way.

> Here's another money conundrum you might relate to. A woman told me, "My mother-in-law expects us to buy Christmas gifts for every single person in my family. There are 15 adults and 20 kids in my family! Every year, my husband's siblings try to change it to a one-gift Secret Santa game, but she refuses. She says that would ruin the spirit of Christmas, but the truth is, I'm just tired of having debt after the holidays every year trying to meet that expectation."

This is definitely a hard one. Anything that has to do with family holidays and money can get tricky. But, I'm with her—having debt after the holidays cancels out any joy gifts might bring. According to a survey, in 2019, Americans took on $1,325 of debt on average during the holidays.[1] Additionally, the same survey reported 78% of people polled said they would not pay off their holiday debt by January.

And, those are just the financial numbers. What's more concerning to me is a different 2019 survey that reported 61% of Americans were dreading the holidays due to the financial burdens the holidays bring. Millennials especially felt this pressure as 71% of them felt obligated to purchase gifts. And, guess who the survey found would struggle the most repaying holiday debt one year later? The answer is millennials and parents of children under 18.[2]

The holidays are not only a financial burden for millennial moms, but they are an incredible source of stress. Do not let other people steal your joy and force you to spend your hard-earned money. You have to step up and be the boss and take a stand against anyone who is trying to put your family in financial distress. I say this as an advocate for moms who have enough on their plates, who have enough bills to worry about. You should not feel obligated to buy a gift for your Great Aunt Beth just because your mother-in-law says you have to.

Save your money throughout the year and enjoy showering your own kids with gifts until you are in a better financial position. There are plenty of other ways to be generous and giving with your family members that don't involve you going into credit card debt for the next year just because you wanted to save face. Remember, the more you plan, save, and invest now, the more generous you can be in the future. I would rather be able to help with big gifts and be outrageously generous with my extended family 10 years from now rather than go into debt now buying gifts kids will stop playing with in a matter of days.

I know this won't be easy. People like the status quo. People like to keep things the way they are. And, when you go in trying to switch up holiday traditions, events, girls nights, or kids' birthday parties, there's going to be somebody who doesn't like it. They might call you Scrooge when you insist on buying one gift for Secret Santa instead of 20 gifts for everyone. However, I guarantee you there are other family members who feel the same way you do. They might even thank you for taking a stand and saving them from having credit card debt for the next year too.

Whenever you find it hard to say no or step into a boss-mom role, think about those beautiful kids of yours. Which is worse: your mother-in-law getting mad at you for not buying a ton of gifts or you putting your finances (and thus, your kids' livelihood) at risk by going further into debt? I don't know about you but I choose my kids every time. If your mother-in-law uninvites you to Christmas because you won't participate in the over-the-top gift giving, I think that's a cause for celebration. You're free! Enjoy a nice quiet Christmas at home with your kids instead.

I've given a few examples of how to overcome financial issues when it comes to extended family relationships and friendships. But the ones that are perhaps the hardest to work through are the ones that happen in your own home.

Before I start, I want to say there's a big difference between couples having arguments about money and financial abuse. Financial abuse is when your partner exercises complete control over the finances and restricts your access to them. It's when they demand you report every single expense and when they get mad if you spend something on yourself or on something you didn't get preapproved by them. It's when your partner refuses to allow you to earn your own money because that means they won't have control over you anymore. If you feel trapped because of financial abuse and feel as though you don't have any autonomy, please put this book down and seek help. Call a licensed counselor who can provide you with resources and next steps to take.

All women, all moms, should have access to money they feel as though they can spend freely without fear of punishment or judgment. And that's true for their partners too. Even if your accounts are completely joined, each person in a relationship should have a set amount of money they can spend each month with no questions asked. It can be as little as $20 if you're in the middle of paying off huge sums of debt or as much as you want if you're in an amazing financial position. Relationships thrive with trust, and if you feel anxious or like you need to hide your purchases because you don't want your partner to get mad at you, something needs to change.

There's even a term called financial infidelity, which means that one partner lies to the other about money. It can be as small as hiding a purchase you know you shouldn't make or as big as hiding large sums of debt or having secret credit cards. This can lead to a lot of money disagreements and mistrust once it comes to light. However, if you're willing to work together, you can overcome it, possibly with the assistance of a marriage counselor, depending on how serious the financial infidelity is.

If you're having more surface-level disagreements about money with your partner, there are a few things you can do. What I mean by surface level are money issues that you would not classify as financial infidelity or financial abuse. It includes things like disagreeing about how much to spend on gifts or one member of the relationship being much more frugal than the other. Perhaps you just have a different way of managing money or saving money and you're finding it hard to get on the same page.

If this is the case, it's important to understand each other's money history first. Talk about what each person's parents taught them about money or what they learned about money growing up.

Here are a list of questions you can ask each other that can start these conversations:

1. Do you think your parents handled money well?
2. What is one thing you think your parents did right when it comes to money and what's one thing you wish they had done differently?
3. Are there any money lessons you learned as a child that you'd like to keep as an adult?
4. Are there any money lessons you learned as a child that you now think are wrong as an adult?
5. What did you learn about wealthy people growing up?
6. What did you learn about the stock market growing up?
7. Growing up, what did you think a rich person looked like?
8. What do you think a rich person looks like now as an adult?
9. Did your parents keep any financial secrets from one another that you know of?
10. What do you think classifies as a financial secret?
11. Were your parents generous with others?
12. What is one thing you wished would have been different when it comes to money during your childhood?
13. What is one thing you would change now when it comes to money?
14. What is one thing you hope to teach your kids about money?
15. What is one thing you think you do well when it comes to money?
16. What is one thing you wish you could do better when it comes to money?

Each one of these questions could be a full conversation, but the goal is to get some perspective on how your partner came to be the way they are when it comes to money. When you come from different upbringings and learn different money lessons, you're bound to have some disagreements about the way things should be done.

The key to success when having these conversations is to first remember that you're on the same team. Hopefully, you've completed the exercise of writing down your biggest money goals that's mentioned earlier in this book. When you have those goals handy, it's a good way to remind each other you're on the same side of the battle. You're putting on the same armor. You want the same big successes for your family.

The other thing to remember is that as long as your disagreements don't qualify as financial abuse, you're in a safe space. This is your partner, your buddy. So, vulnerability should be encouraged and allowed without judgment. Digging into how things were in your childhood can prompt very triggering conversations. That's why it's good to take the questions slowly. But, with each new thing revealed to each other, you can work together on the joint goals you want to set for your family.

When you have these conversations, you can figure out why your partner hates it when you buy generic groceries or why they feel so passionately that you always tip 20% at a restaurant. There are usually reasons behind our money philosophies and decisions, and sharing them can really help you better understand your other half.

This is also a good time for you to do some self-reflection. If you have trouble with impulse shopping, is it because you saw your mom do it? If you hide your shopping purchases in your trunk, is it because you're afraid of confrontation? When you get angry every time you think your partner overspends, is it because you had a dad who overspent? Try to examine your feelings. What are you worried about when it comes to money—security, the future, your kids? And, why do you think those are your primary worries?

Through a lot of conversations, including some sticky ones, I've been able to find a good balance when it comes to talking about money with my husband. You can imagine what it might be like for him to be married to someone who is a financial educator. Super fun, right?

I mean, I like looking at our money every day. We have a shared main checking account, and I'm always tracking our spending and keeping an eye on things. Because I can get a little obsessed with cash flow, budgets, and saving for the future, there are times I'm too overbearing and too focused on the tiny details.

One time, just a few months into our marriage, I asked my husband if he could pay a water bill. We were in a new apartment, and for some reason, I was worried it would be late. So, he agreed to go and pay it in person (at the time, the water company didn't have an online portal). Well, he never did. The check just sat in his car. He had every intention of paying it, of course, but he never got around to it. A few weeks later, I got a letter in the mail saying they were going to cut off our water because we hadn't paid the bill. When he got home, I confronted him and asked him if he paid it, and he very earnestly told me yes. Then, I held the letter up, and he had to admit he hadn't paid it at all.

My husband is usually one of the most honest Boy Scouts around, so I was really confused why he would lie about the water bill. Eventually, it came out that he didn't want to disappoint me. He felt a lot of shame around the fact that he promised to do something but didn't get around to it. We were newly married in our first place together, and he felt like he had completely failed me as a husband. He didn't want to admit it at first, but when I showed him the letter, he really had no recourse.

I wasn't going to include this story in the book because it doesn't paint him in the best light, but he told me I could. After all, it shows that we're human and that even though we get along pretty well now when it comes to our money, that was not always the case. It took years of us working together through many budget meetings, many setbacks, and many triumphs to get to the place we are today.

One breakthrough that really helped us was setting up separate fun money accounts for each person, money we could spend with no questions asked. I regret that it took us years into marriage to do this, because it really was a huge game changer. I realized that although we share the majority of our earned money, each of us deserves to be able to do a little spending without the other looking over our shoulder.

He needed to have some autonomy and the ability to buy the things he likes guilt-free. I had enough self-awareness to realize he deserved to have some spending privacy away from me and my tendency to want to control everything when it comes to our finances. Neither of us takes advantage of our fun money, and sometimes we even use it to buy gifts for each other. It's been a positive change that has helped us a lot, but we only arrived at it after vulnerable discussions about how each of us felt about our money management and joint money goals.

I do hear from a lot of women who want to improve their finances but they can't get their husbands or partners on board with the plan. They want to budget, save for their kids' college education, and get out of debt. However, their partner just loves buying fishing equipment or hunting gear or power tools (really, insert any expensive hobby).

My advice is always the same. You, unfortunately, cannot force another adult to do what you want with money. You can't nag them into it. You can't aggravate them until they relent. They have to make the choice for themselves. Adults need to feel like they have autonomy and no one wants to feel controlled. It's not healthy. Then again, burning through money isn't a great situation either.

So, what I always say is you have to lead by example. To give an analogy, my husband has recently gotten into fitness ever since he finally graduated from residency and has a more normal schedule. He's been making green smoothies in the morning, going to the gym after work, and doing intermittent fasting. And me, well, I've been drinking a lot of coffee (okay, and ordering the occasional McDonald's fries). But the more my husband keeps talking about how great he feels and how much he loves his smoothies, the more I'm interested in joining him on his journey. The more weight he loses and the more definition he gets in his arms, the more I feel like perhaps I too should go to the gym sometime. He's never once told me to eat the same things as him or told me I should start doing some pushups. But, he's still influencing me because he's the person I interact with the most.

The same is true when it comes to money. When your husband's truck gets a flat tire, and he calls you worried about the cost, present him with your automobile sinking fund envelope. The money is already there. It'll be like giving him a gift. Talk about how much less stress you feel now that you have your initial emergency fund. Decorate the walls with quotes about money and success. Speak positively about your journey, about the progress you've made. Talk about how great it feels to go back-to-school shopping for the kids because you saved for it all summer. Show him the cash you earned from selling things you don't need on your porch. Eventually, slowly but surely, they will come around. They'll join you on the journey. They'll see all the positive changes you're making. For some, the transformation will be quick. Others, who are more stubborn, might take some more time. But, keep trying and keep setting an example. When you don't put pressure on them to be a certain way, sometimes they're more likely to come around.

The last financial relationship I want to mention is your financial relationship with your kids. Kids learn so much from their parents without us explicitly explaining things. They will soak up any money worries or anxieties you have, and they will take your money lessons with them to adulthood just like you took your childhood understanding of money with you to adulthood. So it's important to do some self-reflection and monitor what you say about money knowing the lessons you teach will have an impact on how they handle money in the future.

One of my earliest childhood money memories was asking my mom how much money she made. I have no idea why I asked her the question, but I do remember we were in our parked car while my dad pumped gas. She turned around in her chair slowly and said, "Catherine, that's not really something you ask people. That's actually a very rude question." I remember feeling embarrassed for having asked and quietly trying to blend into the backseat. It was one of the first times I realized money can be a taboo topic. My mom is very elegant and taught me so much about manners, setting the table correctly, and working hard. I'm sure she didn't want me to go around asking her friends that same question at our next social gathering. So I understand. In fact, years later, I found myself in a similar situation while driving to go on a hike with my family.

When my son, who was five at the time, innocently asked me why one of his friends lived in a "dream house" and we didn't, I tried to answer in a way that was educational or would inspire him. On the spot, I responded that his friend's parents were very hard workers. They saved their money for a long time and bought their house. So, I told him, if he wanted to buy a house like that someday, he needed to keep working hard at school and make sure he kept practicing his reading and his math.

Later, as we walked on the trail on our hike and our kids ran ahead, my husband admitted he was frustrated with my response. At the time, he was working nonstop at the hospital with grueling 24-hour call shifts as the chief resident. Medical residents are notoriously overworked and underpaid while they're still in training. In fact, the hike we were on was a bit of a celebration, a reprieve, because it was one of his first days off in a while. "If working hard equated to a dream house," he said, "between the two of us, we'd have a pretty big one right now."

He wasn't wrong. There are millions of hardworking Americans in grueling jobs who don't get paid well enough to own "dream houses." There's also a lot of people who own large, luxurious houses but can't afford them and are mere weeks away from foreclosure. That's hard to explain on the spot to a five-year-old, though. In the end, my goal with my kids isn't to answer their money questions perfectly, because I know I'll make mistakes. The point is to keep an open dialogue so they feel comfortable asking me questions. As time goes on, I can layer on more lessons once they're old enough to understand them.

Connecting work and money, even though it's not a perfect explanation, is still one of my favorite ways to talk to my kids about money. They can learn about working smarter by creating passive income streams, investing, and building businesses as time goes on. But, initially, I want them to connect the idea that when you work, you get paid. When you get paid, you can buy housing, food, clothes, and if you're lucky, some wants too.

If I can teach my kids this lesson and they understand how to go out and work, then I can worry less about them. If they always know that if they want something, they can work to get it, then there's no real reason to ask me for money.

As a parent, my primary goal is to create two humans who are independent citizens. I don't plan on bankrolling their adulthood. I expect both of them to get jobs and pay their bills without asking me for money. When adult children rely on their parents for money or housing (or both), it complicates the relationship. It guilts parents because they don't want their kids to suffer, but it also hurts kids because it prevents them from knowing what it's like to be 100% self-sufficient. I want my kids to be independent not because it makes things easier on me but because it empowers them.

I'd rather have an adult relationship with my children based on generosity than one based on dependence. In other words, I want to give to them from a place of joy and not a place of obligation. In order to create a relationship like that, I know I have to plant the seeds now, while they're young.

I talk to my kids about money quite a bit, and it's something I encourage other parents to do as well. It can be as simple as explaining what you're doing with your money. For example, ever since my kids were babies, I roll down their windows while I pump gas. I always say something like, "Kids, I'm putting gas in the car. I'm putting my debit card into this machine to pay for it. My debit card has money on it because I worked. When I work, I get paid, and that is why we can put gas in the car." As they got older, I'd ask them to predict how much the gas cost, and we'd compare the numbers each week.

Money conversations with your kids don't always have to be serious sit down discussions. You can simply bring it up during your day-to-day activities, like pumping gas. That helps them to know it's okay to talk about money and okay to ask questions about it. I have one friend who only pays for her groceries in cash solely because she wants her daughter to count out the money to pay for their food. Her daughter has been doing this ever since she was four years old. Asking your kids to count out cash is a great, tangible way to help them understand that you actually have to part with money to get an item in exchange.

As I mentioned previously, though, kids will pick up on money lessons even if you don't explicitly teach them. For example, I watched my mom save cash envelopes for a variety of activities and family vacations. She never told me explicitly, "Hi! Look at what I'm doing! I'm organizing my cash!" But I watched her do it so many times, I soaked up the lesson. I can see very clearly in my mind the spot where she kept the envelopes in the house I grew up in. She also regularly asked us to write checks out for her whether it was for a school activity fee or the book fair.

There are opportunities available all the time to teach your children about money. The goal is to develop a positive relationship with them where neither of you are dependent on the other financially as adults. Teach them how to earn money on their own, be generous with them when they become independent, and help them to form positive associations between work and money.

Most importantly, be mindful of how you talk about money and let them know they can work for anything they desire. My son is absolutely a car guy, and he's enamored with the Tesla Model X because of the Falcon Wing doors. I mean, what's not to like? Instead of saying how expensive that car is or telling him only wealthy people can have that car, I tell him how cool it will be when he can buy one for himself one day. When he asks me if we can buy one *now*, I simply say, "No, I really like my car, son. I think I'm going to keep it, but you can buy one for yourself when you're big. I can't wait to ride in it."

You have to let kids dream big and teach them the steps to get to where they want to go responsibly. Obviously, my husband and I don't want our kids to be in piles of debt or spend more than they earn. But, they'll get those lessons too. When they're old enough to buy cars and houses, the hope is they'll both be able to self-regulate and have the discipline to buy only what they can truly afford. Perhaps that will be the newest Tesla or maybe a Honda. Either way, we'll be proud, not because of the purchase itself but because of the independent choices they made to arrive at their decisions.

Perhaps the biggest, most important conversation you need to have with your kids is about paying for college. They need to know, early on, whether you're going to pay for some of their college education, all of it, or none of it. There are two main types of college savings plans—the 529 college savings plan and the ESA, which stands for education saving account.

The 529 accounts are tax-advantaged savings accounts. Each state offers one, and the money you contribute to it is typically invested. They are easy to open and contribute to, but speak with a CERTIFIED FINANCIAL PLANNER™ or your accountant to determine which plan is right for you and how contributing to the plan affects your taxes. Sometimes people worry about contributing to college savings plans because it counts as assets and can potentially reduce the amount of student aid your child could get. Speak to a CFP® about your concerns, but ultimately, the goal of parents who save in 529 accounts is to avoid the need for financial aid.

Additionally, 529 accounts and ESAs have different rules and different limits of what you can contribute each year. You can even use the money in them to pay for private elementary school or high school. Don't be intimidated by the fact that these are investment accounts. Ask as many questions as you need about the accounts as not all 529 plans are created equally. Some perform better than others, but either way, the earlier you start the better.

You can also talk to your kids about attending a community college for two years prior to matriculating at a university, which is one great cost savings technique. There are also many trade schools they can attend instead of university that can lead to excellent jobs in the future. If your child is very set on a particular college with a high price tag, make sure they understand the weight of that decision if going there requires they take on significant student loan debt. At 17 or 18, it's hard to conceive of the impact that student loan debt can have on your life. But when you're 25 and have little cash flow due to student loan bills, it makes it hard to pursue other financial goals. It can lead to a lot of regret.

As you can see, having college conversations as early as possible is important. Letting your kids know what you can afford and setting your boundaries and expectations around this topic can help to prevent regret on your part and theirs. After all, you still have to focus on your own investments and retirement goals. You can't risk your own financial future for their college plans, because that could lead to your dependence on them as you age. Plus, in the future, I imagine the college landscape will change.

Who knows what the cost of college will be when my own children are college age. Perhaps more and more people will forgo college in favor of tech certifications as those sectors grow. Either way, I plan to continue to save for my twins to go to college and have these discussions openly with them as we invest for their education. That way, together we can make the best college choices for them for their futures, both in the professional sense and the financial sense.

In sum, when you're on a financial journey, whether you're paying down debt, building wealth, or at a point where you can focus on extreme generosity, your relationships matter. Your communication and openness with others is vital to having healthy ones. It's important to spend time ensuring your relationships with your friends, family, spouse, and children are positive when it comes to the topic of money. It's wise to have people in your life who understand and support where you are on your financial journey.

Your network, your circle of friends, and family members do have an impact on your financial and personal success. Be smart about who you take advice from and who you want to let into your circle of vulnerability when it comes to money.

And if you're reading this thinking you'd love to have more friends, I completely understand. So many moms struggle with finding friends, making friends, and keeping friends because of the extreme demands and constraints that raising children places on their lives.

At the end of the day, good, solid, ride-or-die friendships take time. They take work. They also take a significant amount of vulnerability. I know that now. It's not enough to have surface-level friendship where you just text happy pictures of your kids back and forth. True friends require depth and truth. That level of intimacy takes significant energy, something I know many moms—myself included—have trouble conjuring. But, if this is something that's missing in your life, I encourage you to place a little more focus on building your network of relationships. Reach out to friends you've lost touch with. Say hello to another mom at the park or when you're picking up kids from school. Make the effort and work to build your tribe.

Of course, the hardest part of working on relationships, whether it's with family or friends, is that you will lose some people along the way. You might even have to set up boundaries with people you love very much because they don't respect your money habits or rules.

Talk to anyone who has paid off massive amounts of debt and they'll tell you about people who made fun of them along the way. Ask anyone who built wealth by saying no to common consumer desires or working every weekend building a business, and they'll tell you about people who called them cheap or workaholics. I once had a friend who got upset with me because she invited me to lunch, and I told her I couldn't because I had a meeting with a potential client at the same time. She said, "Don't you have enough clients? Do you really need one more?" Um, yes, I do. It's called running a business.

Because most people have debt and live paycheck to paycheck, it can be alarming for them when someone close to them decides to break the mold. Normally, people don't like people who make them feel less than them. And, even though you might not be trying to, the mere act of doing something different and taking the time to improve yourself can seem like a personal attack to those who aren't quite ready to join you on the journey.

It's unfortunate to admit, but you'll find the more you learn about money and the more you focus on improving your own financial situation, the more awkward it makes other people who are perhaps not quite there yet. And, you can't teach the unwilling.

Still, I get it how they feel. When my kids were babies, I had to unfollow a lot of my mom friends on Facebook and Instagram who had babies the same age as mine. Every time they posted a milestone that my preemie babies hadn't reached yet just highlighted my own insecurities about my parenting and my twins' development. Every time a friend showed family pictures of their kids beautifully dressed in a tidy home amplified the shame I felt about my house being a disaster and my twins running around in only diapers. It was easier at the time to unfollow them than to reach out and share my pain and ask for support and help. Sometimes people just aren't ready, and that's okay.

So, I understand when people unfollow me or give me a hard time for being "too frugal" or "caring about money too much." I've learned their discomfort says a lot more about them than it does about me. And, I know when people want my advice, they'll ask—no need for me to force it on them.

At the end of the day, you have to do what's best not only for your family but for your future legacy. Sometimes that means disappointing people. Sometimes it means inspiring people. It might mean not attending a girl's night because you're trying to pay off your student loans. Perhaps you'll begin by saying no to a family trip because it would put you in debt. It also might mean sending up a boundary and distance from a friend who gives you a hard time about being frugal and finding a new one who is on the same journey. It might mean having a super uncomfortable conversation with your husband to understand what money lessons he learned in childhood and how they impact your marriage today. It could mean letting your child know they might be responsible for a part of their college education.

We all have to make choices about who we let into our lives and who we allow to be privy to our most vulnerable beliefs and choices when it comes to money. But, finding a good tribe of people who will support you in both good times and bad is worth the effort it takes. It's worth the pain of losing people along the way. It's worth the discomfort of disagreeing and arguing with the ones we love, because, at the end of the day, this journey is about you. It's about your growth as a woman, as a mom, and about the massive impact your choices will have on your kids and family in the future. You hold this power in your hands, so choose wisely who accompanies you on your path to financial success.

NOTES

1. Erika Giovanetti, "Americans Racked Up $1,325 in Holiday Debt in 2019—And Most Won't Pay It Off on Time," MagnifyMoney, December 27, 2019, www.magnifymoney.com/blog/news/2019-holiday-debt-survey/.
2. "61% of Americans Are Dreading the Holidays Due to Financial Strain, LendingTree Survey Finds," *PR Newswire*, December 3, 2019, www.prnewswire.com/news-releases/61-of-americans-are-dreading-the-holidays-due-to-financial-strain-lendingtree-survey-finds-300968469.html.

CHAPTER 10

The Art and Joy
of Giving

'd just walked into a coffee shop to sit down and get some writing done (I know; coffee shops are a common theme in this book). And, while I was waiting for my order, something weird happened.

I was overwhelmed with a feeling: *Buy coffee for the girl behind you.*

Instantly, I thought nope, not going to do it. Look, I'm happy to buy someone coffee in the drive-through during the holidays or make an anonymous donation. In person, though? No, thanks. Too awkward.

Buy her the coffee. The feeling seemed to come from outside me, and it was a bit alarming. As a self-employed writer, I've spent thousands of hours doing my work in coffee shops, and not once did I ever feel like I should buy a stranger coffee in person. (It goes against the introvert code.)

So nope, I'm not doing it, I thought.

But then the girl stepped up to the register to pay and my mouth, seemingly without my consent, said, "Oh, I'll get hers too." I handed my card over before she could take hers out. I could feel my heart pounding as I looked over and smiled at her.

"Wow," she said, "Thank you." And, after a brief pause, she seemed to weigh her options and decided to add, "I've actually just had the worst morning of my entire life. I didn't think nice people existed in the world anymore."

And with that, she collected her coffee, turned around, and left.

That same day, when I opened my computer to work, I had an unexpected work opportunity arrive in my inbox after weeks of failing to get new contracts. Sure, it could have been a coincidence, but it's happened to me so many times now that I know it's not.

Throughout this book, I've given you several steps to take to improve your finances. I've shown you sample net worth calculations, a sample budget, and we've talked about emergencies and life insurance. I've shown you the nuts and bolts of how I manage cash flow and my bank accounts. We even dabbled in investing. These are all very straightforward, predictable pieces of money advice.

But, there's something I can't quite explain in words. It's so abstract and definitely not straightforward, practical, or predictable. Yet, I've experienced it many times so I want to share it with you.

Every single time you give away money, I believe you will get it back some way or another.

The key is you have to give money that's untethered, money you don't expect to get back, money that holds no hint of ownership or expectation of reciprocation.

You can't force when it happens, and you can't write a check to someone expecting to find a check of equal value in your mailbox tomorrow. When you truly give from the heart, with pure generosity, the money comes back eventually, sometimes when you least expect it.

I don't know why this works, but I suspect a lot of it has to do with your mind. When you give freely, you send a signal to your brain that you have enough. Not only do you have enough, but you have an abundance, so you don't mind giving some of it away. This opens you up for new opportunities and puts you at a different frequency.

It's when you're scared and feeling scarce, clinging to your money, that the problems arrive. When I think back to the times in my life when I was so worried about money, I see now why I felt like I couldn't get ahead. All I did in those dark times was worry about paying my bills and making sure my business grew. I used to take any freelance job I could, even if it didn't pay well, because I didn't believe other gigs were out there. I didn't want to do anything fun; I thought everything was too expensive. And, like many women, I was conditioned to believe that I should be grateful for what I had and not demand more. This kept me in a cycle of working for too little pay. It didn't help my confidence, and I wasn't sending the right signals out into the world.

I would have been stuck in that cycle for years had I not started doing more personal development, therapy, and finding mentors I admired. I realized that a scarcity mindset is connected to self-worth. I had to start appreciating my own work ethic and recognizing my own gifts before I realized the world is an abundant place. I began to believe clients were lucky to work with someone like me. I started to believe the world will never run out of opportunities. And because opportunities for growth and wealth building will always be there, there's no reason why I shouldn't give when I feel called to do so. After all, the money will come back to me, and I can always create more of it. So, why not give some of it away when I want to, right?

I feel that giving is really similar to budgeting in a way. When you learn how to manage a small amount of money, it's a lot easier to manage a large amount of money. Similarly, I feel like when you learn how to give with small amounts of money, it trains you to incorporate giving as a part of your daily life. That way, as you grow, progress in life, and build wealth, you're going to be even more generous in the future.

I haven't given away thousands of dollars at one time yet. I don't have any buildings named after me yet. But, I still have fun giving what I can. Lots of people think they have to have a lot of money to be generous, but that's just not true. You don't have to be a multimillionaire to make a difference when it comes to giving. A simple coffee will do, as evidenced by the story at the beginning of this chapter.

You can even make giving a line item in your budget. My best friend and her husband set aside money every month for surprise giving. It's anywhere from $50–$100 every month. Sometimes they use it right away. Other times, they let the fund build up until they feel called to use it. Once, they bought another couple's Valentine's Day dinner at a restaurant just to be nice. Another time, they helped a single mom at their church who was experiencing a hard time. I love their method of including giving in their budget because it keeps the possibility in the forefront of their minds. It's not something they do for recognition or because they expect something in return. It's pure fun for them, and I love hearing how they use it.

You can do something similar today. Simply go to the ATM and pull out a $20 bill. Put it in your wallet in a different section and call it your "giving money." You'll be surprised at how quickly you'll spot an opportunity to use it, whether the person in front of you at the grocery store forgot her wallet or you decide to give your hairdresser an extra tip. People experience such joy with the smallest gestures. Recently, my friend surprised my family with donuts one morning, and it made our day. I thought it was such a good idea, the following week I put a box of donuts on the porch of another friend who had to quarantine for Covid-19. That made *her* day. That's another thing about generosity: it's infectious (the good kind of infectious, not the pandemic kind of infectious).

Small acts of kindness and surprise giving are truly my favorite form of generosity. I love how it brightens a stranger's day and impacts people I know and love right away. You can, of course, give in a multitude of ways, and giving to organizations is a part of that as well.

If you want to give to a charity organization, you might be wondering how to find one that will use your donated money wisely. You can research charities on a website called Charity Navigator, which rates 501(c)(3) public charities. These charities file an IRS form called Form 990, which Charity Navigator uses to rate them based on their financial health and financial transparency. Additionally, nonprofits have to be in operation for a minimum of seven years and generate $1 million or more in revenue for two or more years in order to be rated. So although not every charity will qualify to be rated on Charity Navigator, it's a good place to start to begin learning about organizations that might support causes you believe in.

You can even formalize your giving further and plan to regularly give to a 501(c)(3) charity by opening something called a donor-advised fund. This is a tax-advantaged account you can open and add money to that you want to donate. When you place money into the fund, you can get a tax deduction for that calendar year. You can then donate it to a qualified charity that year or you can invest it so it can potentially grow and allow for more giving down the road. Some DAF funds have minimums to open the account and some don't. An accountant can help you determine whether or not a DAF is right for your tax planning and philanthropic goals.

Many people want to know if they should be charitable while they are paying off debt. My answer is yes. Maybe it doesn't make sense mathematically on paper because you likely want to allocate all your available resources to destroying debt as quickly as possible. But, for those intangible reasons I listed at the beginning of the chapter, I think giving is important for how it makes you feel and for how it reinforces that you're going to be okay.

Whether it's giving a 10% tithe to your church, buying lunch for a friend, or buying gifts for a family in need during the holidays, giving—even when you're in debt—is important for your own spirit and humanity. It reinforces that even though you may have the burden of debt, there are still others less fortunate who could benefit from your help. Again, you don't have to donate thousands of dollars or set up a donor-advised fund if you're currently focused on aggressively paying off debt. But, keep your mind open to the possibility of acts of generosity and look for ways to help others. Remember, the money and the kindness will come back to you in some way or another.

You can also incorporate giving in your money lessons for your kids. Allow them a way to earn money or to keep money gifted to them. Then, you can ask them to divide their money into three categories: spend, save, and give. When their giving jar grows, you can encourage them to choose a charity they believe in. For example, let's say your child has $10 in their giving jar. If they love dogs, you can take them to give their $10 to a local animal shelter. Or, you can take them to a pet store, buy $10 of dog treats or toys, and then take them to the shelter to donate it. It's good to show them tangible ways of giving first, where they can feel good about helping others. It keeps them aware that other people (or animals) benefit from help and generosity. You can even offer to match money in their giving jars, which can provide them with more opportunities to help in a meaningful way.

Kids are actually excellent givers. They haven't experienced financial pitfalls of friends not paying them back or recessions just yet, so they instinctively have an abundance mindset, especially if you've outlined a way for them to earn money or keep money they're gifted.

I love seeing what my kids do with their money. One of the sweetest giving moments I've witnessed happened when I finished my first draft of this book. I told my daughter I finished writing it, and she went to her money jar and brought me back several bills. She reminded me about a "MAMA" necklace I said I liked in a store several weeks earlier but didn't buy for myself. She was insistent I use her money to buy it as a reward for finishing my book. I was so touched she remembered and that she was willing to part with her own money to buy something for me. So, I did buy the "MAMA" necklace, and I wore it in my author photo for this book. It's now one of my favorite possessions. That's the fun part of teaching your kids to be generous. Sometimes, you get to experience the joy of having it reflected back on you.

Ultimately, it's good for kids, especially those with roofs over their heads and food in their bellies, to practice gratitude and to give back. Giving instills kindness in them and can help foster a sense of contentment, which is a key emotion to harness when it comes to successful money management.

Teaching your children to give will take time and effort on your part, especially if you help them earn money, organize their money, and find places to donate their money. However, it's time well spent and can help create hardworking, thoughtful children who were taught to give back from a young age.

I think what I hope the most for you, though, when it comes to generosity is that you start to become generous with yourself. And, by that I don't mean treating yourself to something new at the mall. I mean giving yourself the gift of compassion and kindness as you begin to learn more about money. Being generous with yourself means carving out the time to learn. It's doing whatever you can to ensure you protect yourself financially today and in the future.

Being generous with yourself means that every day you take a moment to feel gratitude and a deep sense of contentment for everything you've experienced thus far and everything to come. It's giving yourself peace and the courage to let go of mistakes you've been holding on to.

When you're generous with yourself, you choose kindness and make a deal with yourself that you won't chastise yourself for past decisions. You let them go, and you don't invite the negative thoughts back. Instead, you reward yourself and lavish yourself with praise for everything you're doing now to create financial peace in your life.

I want you to pursue contentment and cease comparisons with others you believe are further along than you. Soak in a feeling of contentment and love every time you get to kiss your child's head and smell their smell. As my dad once told me, "Don't get it twisted. Success isn't just about money. It's about those two little individuals you're raising." So, have a deep belief that you're exactly where you should be. You've become the person you were meant to be until now. And, everything that's happened thus far in your life has led you to today.

I want you to love yourself and care for yourself so much that even if you're scared to talk about money, you take a seat at the table. You keep trying. You keep budgeting. You keep asking the hard questions, even if the person you're asking doesn't seem like they want to take the time to answer. If you fail, you rest and take a seat again the following day with gratitude for the lessons you've learned.

Being generous with yourself means making a call with an attorney and creating a will, gifting yourself the peace of mind you crave. It means making sure you have investments and retirement accounts in your name, showing respect and honoring future you who might need them. It's researching college savings plans for your children, even if it seems intimidating, because it makes *you* feel accomplished.

It's booking an appointment with a therapist, not because someone else told you to, but because it's a gift to yourself to help you unpack any past trauma. It's agreeing that you want to do the hard work and explore what might be holding you back from pursuing wealth, earning more, or accomplishing some of your biggest, most audacious goals.

Being generous with yourself means assigning the dishes to someone else so you can put your feet up and spend an evening reading and learning in your bed, surrounded by a candle and a hot cup of tea. It's recognizing that you, too, are deserving of some downtime.

When you acknowledge your own needs and desires, you're being true to yourself. When you choose to budget in a babysitter, even if others consider it superfluous, that's showing kindness to yourself and prioritizing your own needs.

You're generous to yourself when you recognize your own value, when you start to believe deep within your soul that you're worthy of your desires, of a raise, and of a packed bank account.

Be generous if an idea comes to your mind for a new product, a new business, or a new way of doing things. Try not to instantly talk yourself out of your ideas or wonder what would happen to your family or your kids if you made it big. Allow yourself a moment to imagine or dream of new possibilities. Recognize that things don't always have to be the same. Sometimes change is a welcome reprieve from a life that is not serving you.

Mostly, be generous with yourself if you make mistakes, if you flounder, or if you fail. Accept the lessons that happen along the way with grace and gratitude, knowing they are helping you to arrive at the place you were always meant to be.

And just know, even if your child woke you up five times last night, even if you showed up to a meeting wearing two different shoes, and even if you forgot to save for something big, you are a boss. You are a warrior who is powerful and influential always and forever, because you are a mom. And, if there is anyone on the planet who can figure out money, it's you.

Start today. Start now. It's you who gets to change your family legacy, to mark a new path. They'll remember you always because you took a chance, you decided to get uncomfortable, and you decided to learn.

Your new money journey starts now with the best possible woman leading the charge, rallying the troops, and saving the day.

It's you, Mama. It's always been you.

Epilogue: Action Steps

Now that you're finished reading *Mom's Got Money*, my greatest hope is that you're fired up and ready to take action. If you don't know where to start, I've included action steps for each chapter here. Good luck on your journey to becoming a boss with your money. You've got this!

You can find these action steps and other free downloads to help you on your money journey at www.momsgotmoney.com.

Action Steps

Chapter 1: Shifting to a Boss Mindset

- Take the time for self-reflection and acknowledge your money fears and worries. Commit to developing a boss mindset and learning all you can about your finances.
- Practice replacing thoughts of overwhelm with empowering ones using the chart in Chapter 1.

Chapter 2: How to Determine Your Household Net Worth

- Find out your household net worth using the examples in Chapter 2 as a formula.
- Analyze where you stand and start to formulate a plan to raise your net worth in the future.

Chapter 3: The Family Budget Meeting

- Write down your biggest goals and dreams for the future. If you have a partner you will be budgeting with, have them do the same.
- Review spending from previous months to find out your budget categories.
- Find out your exact household take-home pay.
- Set the date for a family budget meeting.
- Write your budget, allocating your income to all the various budget categories you have.
- If you don't have enough income to cover all your budget categories, discuss ways you will cut back and earn more.

- If you have excess income after allocating your money to your budget categories, discuss how you will use it toward savings goals and investing.

Chapter 4: How to Manage Your Household Cash Flow and Start Saving

- Review the three budget anchors: house, cars, and food.
- Take action if you find you need to reduce one of your budget anchors, like downgrading your car, downsizing your home, or starting a meal plan.
- Start to shift your bills to a one-month-ahead system using the ROADSS formula outlined in this chapter.
- Once you are one month ahead, automate your bills to free up your mental space.

Chapter 5: How to Increase and Maintain Your Credit Score

- Pull your credit report for free at www.AnnualCreditReport.com.
- Look for mistakes on your credit report. If you find them, dispute them.
- Look for adverse accounts on your credit report. If you see some, make sure they're yours and if they are, call the number listed next to the account to work out a plan to get those accounts current. (Never give a collector access to your checking account. Instead, work out a payment plan or a lower, lump sum payment agreement. Have them send you the agreement in writing.)
- If you have credit card debt, work hard to get that balance under 30% usage (and eventually to 0% usage).
- Strive to pay your bills on time every time.
- Sign up for free credit monitoring at a website like Credit Sesame or Credit Karma.
- Continue to monitor your score, pay bills on time, and pay down debt. Stay informed and vigilant. Empower yourself to raise and maintain your score with positive habits.
- Most importantly, remember that a credit score is just a number, and it says nothing about you or the person you are.

Chapter 6: How to Negotiate, Earn Extra Money, and Start Investing

- Do some self-reflection to identify how you actually feel about money and wealth. What's stopping you from becoming wealthy? What are some positive things you'd be able to do if you had more money?

- Practice negotiating by calling your service providers and asking them to lower your bills.

- Spend time thinking of ways to earn more. For example, set up a meeting with your boss at work to discuss what you can do to earn a raise in the future. Consider starting a side hustle or a business. Remind yourself regularly about your value in this world.

- Read an introductory investing book. Learn about the stock market. Start with a simple, straightforward investment like buying an index fund and build your confidence from there. Remind yourself there's nothing harder than raising kids. Investing is simple compared to motherhood.

- If you have a financial advisor, make sure they are a fiduciary. Ask all your questions, even the ones you feel silly asking. Take a seat at the table, and don't stop trying until you understand how to invest and why it's important for your future.

- Refer to the Old Thoughts/New Thoughts chart in this chapter any time you need help reframing your money thoughts.

Chapter 7: Protect Your Family with Emergency Funds and Insurance

- Start your emergency fund today in a separate account.

- If you have high-interest debt, like credit card debt, start with an emergency fund equal to one month of expenses. Then, kill your credit card debt, and go back to filling up the fund to six-plus months.

- If you have no debt or low-interest debt like student loans or a mortgage, build your emergency fund to six-plus months of expenses.

- Buy *term* life insurance, *not* whole life or any other kind. Insurance is insurance, not an investment account.

- Get a will.
- Create an emergency binder.

Chapter 8: The Childcare versus Career Dilemma

- If you are working and considering becoming a stay-at-home mom, know all of your numbers, especially your gross income and the total value of your benefits. Then, compare that to the cost of childcare and make your decision.

- If you're a stay-at-home mom considering going to work part-time or full-time, run childcare cost numbers. Additionally, don't forget to consider a potential increase in the amount of money you'll spend on outsourcing food, after school responsibilities, and more.

- When running the numbers in either scenario, think ahead to when your children are older and interested in extracurricular activities. Depending on your involvement in them, extracurriculars can get very expensive quickly.

Chapter 9: Finances in Your Relationships

- Be vulnerable with those closest to you about your money dreams and your money concerns, even if it means you might potentially lose them along the way. Vulnerability gives you power and has the potential to deepen your relationships.

- If you think you might be a victim of financial abuse, seek immediate help from a licensed counselor.

- Refer to the list of questions in this chapter for couples and answer them together.

- Research options for saving for college, like ESAs and 529 plans. Be open with your child about what you can contribute.

Chapter 10: The Art and Joy of Giving

- Take $20 out of the ATM and put it in a separate spot in your wallet. Look for opportunities to give on a small scale.

- Research charities on Charity Navigator to find one that fits your interests.

- Encourage your children to split their money into spend, save, and give categories.
- Research donor-advised funds to see if opening one would fit in with your tax planning and philanthropy goals.
- Be generous with yourself. Give yourself time to learn. Be your own cheerleader along your money journey because you *are* a boss deserving of a beautiful, financially secure life.

Index